CAVALRY CHARGE NEAR BRANDY STATION, VIRGINIA 1864

SADDLE AND SABER

The Letters of Civil War Cavalryman
Corporal Nelson Taylor
Ninth New York State Volunteer Cavalry
to
His Father, Shubael Taylor and Sister, Hannah
Clifton Park, New York

November 14, 1861–October 30, 1864

NINTH REGIMENT
NEW YORK VOLUNTEER CAVALRY
THIRD BATTALION
FIFTH SQUADRON
COMPANY I

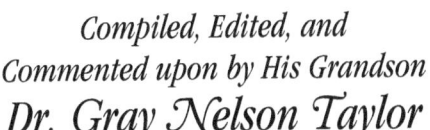

*Compiled, Edited, and
Commented upon by His Grandson*
Dr. Gray Nelson Taylor

HERITAGE BOOKS
2011

HERITAGE BOOKS
AN IMPRINT OF HERITAGE BOOKS, INC.

Books, CDs, and more—Worldwide

For our listing of thousands of titles see our website at
www.HeritageBooks.com

Published 2011 by
HERITAGE BOOKS, INC.
Publishing Division
100 Railroad Ave. #104
Westminster, Maryland 21157

Copyright © 1993 Gray Nelson Taylor

On the cover:
General Buford's Engagement with Stuart's Confederate Cavalry at Boonsboro, Maryland, July 9, 1863

All rights reserved. No part of this book may be reproduced or transmitted in any form or by any means, electronic or mechanical, including photocopying, recording or by any information storage and retrieval system without written permission from the author, except for the inclusion of brief quotations in a review.

International Standard Book Numbers
Paperbound: 978-1-55613-847-8
Clothbound: 978-0-7884-8673-9

ACKNOWLEDGMENTS

Transcribing over one hundred of Grandfather Nelson Taylor's letters written while a Civil War Cavalryman serving with the Ninth New York State Volunteer Cavalry was a daunting task.

The editor is grateful for the steadfast encouragement and constructive comments of his wife, Georgiana; his four children; Grandfather Nelson's other grandson, Willard Taylor; and numerous friends interested in Civil War history.

Diligent effort was made to determine copyright ownership through publishers, the United States Copyright Office, and the Library of Congress.

The cover illustration is from a sketch by C. E. H. Bonwill appearing in Vol. II of an 1886 book entitled The Soldier in Our Civil War edited by Paul F. Mottelay and T. Campbell-Copeland. The volume was entered in the Office of the Librarian of Congress 1885, and published by G. W. Carleton & Company, New York.

In describing the movements of the 9th NY Cavalry, the editor relied heavily on the History of the Ninth New York Cavalry, by Newell Cheney, Captain and Brevet Major, published by Martin Merz & Son, Jamestown, N.Y., 1901.

PLATE I is from Cheney cited above.

The etchings for the frontispiece and PLATES V-VII and IX-XIV appear in a 1957 volume entitled A Civil War Artist at the Front, Edwin Forbes' Life Studies of the Great Army, edited by William Dawson and published by Oxford University Press. Forbes' originals reside in the Library of Congress.

CONTENTS

TITLE PAGE i
ACKNOWLEDGMENTS. iii
PHOTOGRAPHS AND ILLUSTRATIONS. vii
INTRODUCTION ix
WESTFIELD TO ALBANY. 1
CAMP FENTON, WASHINGTON, DC 3
MOVING WITH McCLELLAN'S ARMY 23
HOSPITALIZED WITH TYPHOID. 47
ON POPE'S CAMPAIGN 59
DEFENDING WASHINGTON 67
FREDERICKSBURG 77
CHANCELLORSVILLE 85
GETTYSBURG CAMPAIGN. 93
AFTER GETTYSBURG 99
WINTER 1863-64, KILPATRICK'S RAID. 115
GRANT AND SHERIDAN 135
THE WILDERNESS, SPOTTSYLVANIA, JAMES RIVER .141
TREVILLIAN STATION RAID. 155
SHENANDOAH VALLEY CAMPAIGN 171
APPENDIX 187
    AFTERTHOUGHT (After Discharge). 187
    FROM TAYLOR FAMILY RECORDS. 199
    SOURCE MATERIALS. 201
    NEIGHBORS AND FRIENDS MENTIONED 203

PHOTOGRAPHS AND ILLUSTRATIONS

PLATE	I	Arms Carried by the 9th NY Cavalry
"	II	Nelson Taylor at Enlistment
"	III	Shubael Taylor, Nelson's Father
"	IV	Alida Teachout Taylor, Nelson's Mother
"	V	Fall in for Soup
"	VI	A Cavalry Charge
"	VII	Winter Camp
"	VIII	Daguerreotype of Corporal Nelson Taylor
"	IX	An Advance of the Cavalry
"	X	The Pontoon Bridge
"	XI	The Supply Train
"	XII	The Picket Line
"	XIII	A Christmas Dinner
"	XIV	Through the Wilderness
"	XV	Wedding Photo of Nelson Taylor and Alida Teachout
"	XVI	Gloversville, NY Chief of Police Nelson Taylor
"	XVII	Gloversville Police Force Heading a Funeral Procession - Chief Nelson Taylor at Left

PLATE I

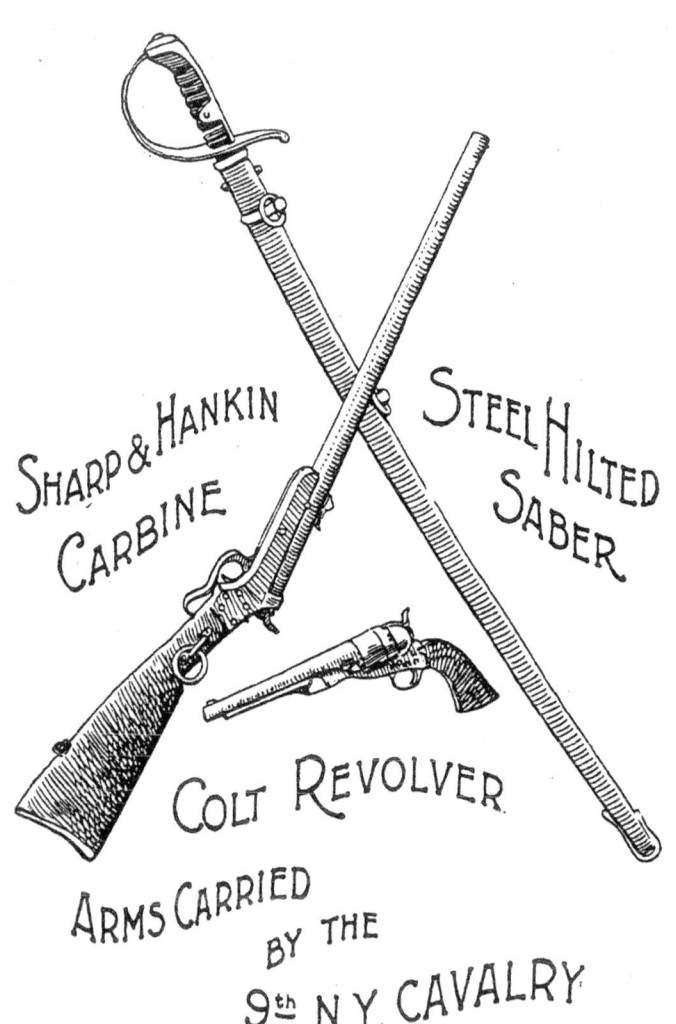

INTRODUCTION

Corporal Nelson Taylor served as a cavalryman with the 9th New York State Volunteer Cavalry from his enlistment on September 10, 1861 at age 22, to his honorable discharge on October 25, 1864. During those three years he wrote with great regularity to his father, Shubael Taylor; to his sister, Hannah; and occasionally to his cousin, Mary; all living in Clifton Park, New York, close to Albany. Shubael was a prosperous farmer who maintained a large farm. One hundred of Nelson's letters were lovingly preserved by his family and were handed down to one of Nelson's sons, my father, Charles; thence to me, Nelson's grandson, Gray Nelson Taylor.

Nelson was the last of six children born to Shubael Taylor and his wife, Alida Teachout Taylor. Nelson had two brothers: John S., and George W. John and George were married with children and were well-established on large-acreage farms. There were three sisters: Lydia, Loantha, and Hannah.

Nelson's education probably was sporadic with regular attendance limited to the winter months. During the remainder of the year, Nelson was frequently needed for farm work. His limited elementary education is reflected in his letters: punctuation is scarce; capitalization is whimsical; spelling is often phonetic; good grammatical construction is not observed.

Acknowledging this, the editor seriously considered correcting the punctuation and spelling and altering the structure to conform to today's grammar edicts. To that end, several of Nelson's letters were revamped. Immediately, however, they ceased to be **his** letters. They became a third party's, watered down, diluted. Tampering with them seemed sacrilegious. Their integrity, authenticity, and "flavor" demand respect. Therefore, Corporal Nelson Taylor's letters are offered in this volume pure and unadulterated. Occasional copies of the originals in Grandfather's hand are included to remind the reader that the letters were really written on the spot by a flesh-and-blood cavalryman.

Understanding of the times and the turbulent forces at work will be enhanced if we pause for a bit of historical comment before we move on to the stage for what follows.

When Abraham Lincoln was elected president in 1860, the Southerners feared the downfall of their way of life. In December of that year, South Carolina seceded, followed by Mississippi, Florida, Alabama, Georgia, and Louisiana. In February of 1861, Jefferson Davis was elected by the seceded states to be President of the Confederate States of America. On March 6, he called for 100,000 volunteers to serve one year as militia, and the Confederacy seized Federal military installations and arsenals. Then on April 12, a Southern cannon fired the first shot of the Civil War at Fort Sumter.

President Lincoln immediately issued a proclamation calling for 75,000 militia for three months' service to suppress the rebellion. Lincoln's call moved Virginia, North Carolina, Tennessee, and Arkansas to join the Confederacy. The western part of Virginia broke away from the rest of the state and stayed with the Union becoming the state of West Virginia finally admitted to the Union in 1863. So now 11 Southern states were arrayed against 23 Northern ones.

The volunteers called for by Lincoln were discharged at the end of their three months' service. However, a large portion of the men re-enlisted in regiments organizing for the three years' service set forth in the President's proclamation of May 3, calling for 42,034 volunteers. In addition, eight regiments of infantry, one regiment of artillery, and a regiment of cavalry were called for.

In response to President Lincoln's specific request that New York State furnish 15,000 men, Governor Morgan issued a proclamation on July 25, 1861, calling for the volunteer force and set up rendezvous at New York, Albany, and Elmira.

Feeling was intense in the northern states and applications for authority to raise troops were numerous. Volunteering was widespread; enthusiasm was whipped up by the war; meetings were held in every town. Because of the flood of requests for authority to raise troops, the State military department established branch depots for organization of regiments. Between August 23 and November 2, twenty-four such branch depots were established, among them the Albany depot.

The Ninth New York Volunteer Cavalry began its organization in September of 1861 by the volunteering of men for cavalry service in the counties of Chautauqua, Cattaraugus, and Wyoming assembled at Westfield.

Nelson Taylor's first letter follows.

Nov 14 1861
Albany Barracks

Father

I am hear in the stoneman Cavalry regtment from Chautauqua County came hear last sunday and we will stay hear 3 or 4 days yet i would come home if i could but i cant get ayway if you can Come Down do so

from your unworthy son
Nelson Taylor

This letter poses some puzzling questions.

1. Were there letters preceding this one? It is not likely when one considers the care with which the letter above and those following were preserved. Then, too, the tone of this first letter appears to indicate that it is the initial contact with his father after leaving home.

2. Why does he close with the self-effacing words, "from your unworthy son"? Although Nelson was 22 when he enlisted, it would have been important to leave with his father's "blessing." Apparently he departed without this approval. At the time of his son's enlistment, Shubael was 64. Since his two other sons had their own farms and families, in all likelihood he had planned to retire and let Nelson take over the farm. What a shattering of dreams this must have been for Shubael! What a sense of guilt must have burdened Nelson! In the closing of his letter, he acknowledges this, and in a roundabout way seems to be asking for forgiveness.

3. When and why did Nelson leave the farm? When he was discharged, he did not return to farming. Although he frequently writes of missing things at home, it is not the farm or farm life that he longs for. In January of 1860, Nelson became 21. Perhaps it was then that he faced up to his dislike for farming and determined that now he was his own man and would so assert. However, his enlistment is dated nearly twenty months later - September 10, 1861. It is quite probable that he headed west in the early summer of 1861.

4. Why did Nelson enlist in the westernmost part of New York State? The official records show that Nelson enlisted at Ripley, in Chautauqua County, on the shore of Lake Erie. Why go clear across the state when there was an enlistment depot in Albany less than 15 miles from home? It does not appear that he left home fired up to enlist, but was heading for the West, the land of opportunity.

The Erie Canal was humming with activity; it was the main thoroughfare from east to west in the state; the Canal was within walking diatance from the three Taylor farms in Clifton Park. Undoubtedly, Shubael and his two older sons, John and George, had shipped produce westward and south to the City. Because of this familiarity, it would have been logical for Nelson to have worked his way to Buffalo on the canal as a mule driver and deckhand.

But what happened when he got as far as Ripley in the extreme southwestern part of the state? Is it too far-fetched to assume that he ran out of money, got caught up in the Civil War patriotic fervor, and saw a three year hitch as a way to mend his fortunes a bit and continue his journey westward upon discharge? He knew and loved horses, so it's understandable that he would volunteer for this branch of the service. The infantry or the artillery were not for him - he was captured by the thought of himself a cavalryman on a mount, in uniform, and brandishing a saber!

PLATE II

NELSON TAYLOR AT ENLISTMENT

PLATE III

SHUBAEL TAYLOR, NELSON'S FATHER

PLATE IV

ALIDA TEACHOUT TAYLOR, NELSON'S MOTHER

WESTFIELD TO ALBANY

Now let's resume our reading of Nelson's letters. The next one was written one week later.

Albany Nov 21

Dear Father
I saw the Docktor this morning again and he said there was no way to get out of this he went to the Adutant Genaral ofice and he said he could not release me But i will Doo the best I can now to make my self contented We will leave here next monday so the Capton said so this morning And if we do go monday I dont think I can come home but if I can come before I leave I will do so
I will take that money you let me have last sunday with me for they wont pay us before we leave hear I wrote a letter too Newton Royce the man that I left my Clothes with and I wrote him to box them up and seend them by express to Waterford and I tould him to write you a line when he sent them I believe i have got all of the Clothing i shall need i have got as much as i can carry with me

Nelson Taylor

The hint of disenchantment enters this second letter with the comment on attempting to get out of the service. Why? Again we can only speculate. Perhaps his patriotic ardor cooled when he experienced some of the realities of life in the armed services. He undoubtedly had a healthy appetite and missed his mother's ample home-cooked farmfare. Conceivably he was just plain homesick, not only for his mother's cooking, but the farm, his friends, and the small town he had left.

The armed services' penchant for nourishing rumor is well known. The government was having great difficulty procuring supplies and mounts, and this word may have been circulating. The volunteers might end up in the infantry or artillery after all, and this was an unthinkable fate. No horse, no sabre - what a prospect!

It's altogether possible that his inquiries of the doctor and adjutant were half-hearted and at the urging of his father. At any rate, Nelson seems to have been easily reconciled to staying in.

From the comment about the "money you let me have last Sunday," we may assume that Father did respond to Nelson's invitation to visit him in Albany. It is not too much to hope that there was a measure of reconciliation. Note that his salutation in the November 21 letter is "Dear Father."

Albany Nov 24

Dear Father

I am well at present and I hope thees few lines will find you the same we leave hear for Washington to morrow night monday night

George Ester and marsha was stop hear friday I would of come home last night if I could but I could not get away The American Tract Scocity Presented evry man in regitmant with a Testament to day I will write to you again as son as we get to Washington

Nelson Taylor

CAMP FENTON, WASHINGTON DC
December 1, 1861 - March 14, 1862

The regiment of some 1,000 officers and men left Albany the evening of November 26, 1861 by the steamer Knickerbocker down the Hudson. They landed at Jersey City on November 27 and that evening boarded another boat for South Amboy. Here they took cars for Washington by way of Philadelphia, Wilmington, and Baltimore.

Travel accommodations were Spartan. Box cars and cattle cars were furnished for the men with rough boards laid on blocks for seats. A passenger coach was attached to the rear of the train for the officers. However, before the train started, one of the soldiers surreptitiously pulled the coupling pin detaching the coach bearing most of the officers, and the train proceeded without them! A few of the officers had stayed with their men sharing the discomforts of the box and cattle cars. The train arrived at Philadelphia about one o'clock on the morning of November 28, and the officers who had been left behind arrived near daybreak.

Records indicate that the soldiers were provided with an excellent supper at the Cooper Shop bearing the sign "Soldiers' Eating Committee Saloon." All soldiers passing through the city were fed free by the citizens' committee at any hour of the day or night.

The train arrived in Washington early Friday morning, and the regiment had breakfast consisting of a chunk of bread, a chunk of boiled beef, and a tin cup of coffee. The tables were bare, and since no eating utensils were provided, the men ate with teeth and fingers. Dinner was bowls of soup with bread.

The regiment marched up Pennsylvania Avenue and pitched tents on Meridian Hill to the north of and overlooking the city. Nelson relates some of this in his December 1 letter.

The encampment was named Camp Fenton in honor of Congressman Reuben E. Fenton. A letter from another soldier states that "Camp Fenton is a healthy place with a good well of water...A few of the men are unwell with colds and the measles, but most of us are flourishing finely on bread, beef, pork, potatoes, coffee, sugar, and molasses."

As Nelson notes in his letter of December 7, when the regiment was en route from New York, some of the men contracted measles; a few were left at Philadelphia to rejoin the regiment as soon as they recovered. There were several deaths at Camp Fenton because the regimental hospital tents could not provide proper care.

                              Washington Dec 1st 1861

Dear Father

    We left Albany Tuesday 3 oclock and we got in to New York the next morning at 8 oclock I saw Able there a few moments then we change boats and went Down to Amboy then we took the cars for this city We arived in Washington Friday morning 5 oclock And then we march out of the city 2 miles on to a sidehill and pitched our tents where we can look over the city They are expecting a battle at Richmond now every day down the Potmack Ther was 40,000 Troops sent across the river from here Thursday and 30,000 yesterday we have not got our horses nor any arms yet we will stay here some time Perhaps a month I am well and have enought to eat write soon from your son

                                      N Taylor

Direct your letter to
Nelson Taylor
in care Capt H J Cowden
Company I 9 Cavalry Regt
N Y S V Camp Fenton
Washington DC

Washington Dec 7th 1861

Dear Father
I wrote you a letter last sunday did you get it I have had a cold for the past 3 days but I am nearly over it now. I thought I was going to have the measels but I hope not there is over 50 got in now in the regitment now and there was 10 takeing down with it before we got to Philadelphia and they was left there we heard from them yesterday they was doing well our Capton was one of them there is a report that our regtiment is a going to be disbanded the sectetary of war recomends to not have any more cavalry Regtiments equipt for there is more in the field now than there is a call for there is something like 12 Regtments here now some of them has been here 2 months and they have not been equiped yet our Col said yesterday he thought it was more likely that we should be disbanded than we would be armed an equiped he said we would know by the 20 how it would be If they do disband our regiment they will get all to enlist in infantry and artileary that they

can but I know of one that dont enlist again
  Col James McKeean of the 67 Rgt is in camt ¼ of a mile frome here I was over there a little wile last monday and I saw Levi Clapper and the to Simmons boys the rest of the boys that I knew was of some where and I did not see them
  Direct your letter to
Nelson Taylor
care Capt H J Cowden
9 Cavalry Regt NYSV
Camp Fenton Washington DC

    Washington Dec 14th 1861
Cos Mary
  I intend to write you a long letter if i dont get tired out before i get through the first thing is the last letter I wrote to father I said that i had a could for 3 or 4 days and I thought I was nearly over it but the next morning that was Sunday norning I comenced brakeing out with the Measels and I went into the Hospital tent it is a tent 16 ft long 12 ft wide with good bunks into it and a small stove and it is warm and nice they broke out firstrate and i was pretty sick for 2 days but I did not have it as hard as some did that was in the tent with me there was 10 in the tent together they took good care of us but not as good as I

would of had if I had been at mother I will get along now if I am careful not to catch any could I am out around now the wether is warm and nice here it seems more like the 14 of June than it does like December there was 4 or 5 days when we first came hear was could and windy we have ocasionly a frost but when the sun gets up it is warm again Mother wanted to know about our washing there is 4 men that brought there wives with them and they do all of the washing they can they wash woolon for 4 ct apice. I let them do my washing that is cheaper than I can do it myself We are in tents 8 ft long 7 ft wide and there is 5 of us in a tent now we lack 2 tents we are alowed a tent for evry 4 men and now I will tell you how we get our grub There is 3 men detaild out of our company to do the coocking for 10 days at a time our stove is a hole dug 1½ ft wide with a crotch drove in each end and a pole laid across we have kettles and stew pans we have fresh beef pork bacon potatoes beans rice tea and Coffee and when our dinner is ready we take our plate and cup and go and draw our rations and then we can go where we are a mind to and eat it and you wanted to know how we pased our sundays last sunday we had preaching here in camp one of the Captons preached our Chaplain Rev Mr. Steaver came here

PLATE V

FALL IN FOR SOUP

yesterday I supose he will preach to us to morrow It dont seem much like sunday here there is evry thing a going on We have not drawed any pay yet and there is a talk that we will be paid off by the 20 and all of those that wont enlist in to infantry will be sent home for they dont want any more Cavalry our Officers feel real sore they are afraid we will be disbanded but some think they will keep us here a month or 2 and see if there is any use for us
    Nelson Taylor

Camp Fenton is the name of our camp And we draw 1 loffe of bread a day You wanted to know what SV stood for it is State Volunteers

    Camp Fenton Dec 25
Cos Mary Father and Mother
  Tooday is Christmas and I wish that I was there to take Dinner with you but wishing does not do any good Well I had a very good dinner to day I went to the Sutlers store and bought an Aple Pie and some sugar Cake and some Bolonyy Saussage and I Made a cup of Tea and I had a good Christmas Dinner Yesterday the boys that tents with me we went in together and bought a Sheet Iron Stove about the size of a bandbox and it weights 10 lbs pipe

and all and we are living like Pigs in the
Clover now to what we did before We got
along Well enought before nights better
than we did in the daytimes for we have a
plenty of bed Clothes The wether is some
colder now than it has been. We have not
been payd any yet the reglar Pay day is
the 1st of January and then we exspect to
be payed off And then we will know wether
we will be keep or not it was in the
Washington Paper this morning that they
would not be any more Cavalry forces
takeing unless they wer fully armed and
equiped And if York State is a mind to
find out I guess they will manage some way
to keep us There has been 3 deaths in the
Regtiment since we have been here one man
of our Company died last night before last
his name was Albert Wells he had the
meassels in the First place and then he
caught Cold he is to be buried this
afternoon the Company is geting ready now
for the Funiral. he is to be buried
nearly a mile from here and I doo not
attend for it is to much of a walk for me
and it would not be prudant for me to do
so although I feel as well as I ever did
but I have not got my strength yet our
Capton has not got here with us yet but we
exspect him here the last of the week I
Recieved a letter from Able and Lant
Yesterday they wer well the letter was

mailed the 10th and I got it the 24 and I recieved a letter from Louise Walradt last Week I wrote one to her and she answered it very promptly I wrote one to George and one to John and they have not answered it or that is I have not recieved any yet Has Father got over his cold yet and mother how does she get along write as often as you can and tell me all of the news

                      Nelson Taylor

The stove cost 2.75

                Camp Fenton Jan 2nd 1862

Dear Father

    It is some too weeks since I have heard from home or had a letter from you I am well at present and I hope and trust that you are the same yesterday was New Years and the wether was as warm and plesant here as any day as you have there in Indian summer It was warm and smokey and today is cold and windy the wether is very changeble one day warm and plesant and the next cold and windy Day before yesterday we wer mustered for pay and each man had to answer to his name as it was caled from the pay roll And the pay rolls are in the hands of the paymasters and we are exspecting to get our pay now evry day And we exspect to get our discharge at the same time and what make me think so our pay rolls are made out on mustering out

rolls and they read that we are honerably
discharge from the united states servis
And the Capt of Co D told one of his men
that this regt was a good as discharge now
and that we would be on our way home less
than too weeks But it is most to good to
belive I cant hardley belive it but I hope
it is so There is some 200 thousand men
here near the city witch are of not much
use to the goverment as I can see and
Goverment cant run this Army a very long
time if it does she will never get out of
debt. Provissions are very high here and
hay is $40 per ton and the Goverment
horses dont have any more hay than what
they want they look very hard the most of
them There was over 200 horses burnt in
one of the sheds down near the City they
wer Goverment horses I was over in the 77
rgt yesterdy and the boys wer all well
excepting Eli Weeks he has been sick all
the time since he has been here he told me
that he saw Elisha Morse one day down to
the City I think he said it was last week
or the week before I wish he had come out
here I would like to of seen him I guess
he was afraid to get out of the City write
as often as you can
        from your son
                Nelson Taylor

Camp Fenton Jan 18, 1862

Father

I am well at present and I hope you and Mother is the same I supose you are looking for me home but I dont know now when I will come home We got our pay yesterday but we did not hear anything about geting discharge and I begin to think we will have to stay untill the war is ended witch I think will be ended less than 6 months unless England turns in against us but I dont think she will I will send my money home by Express to Waterford as soon as I can get a pass to go down to the City witch will be some time next week When I send it I will write you a letter at the sawme time so you can get it My pay amounted to $48.10 up to the first of Jan they keep back $2.00 a month on our wages. We have had 3 or 4 days of winter wether that is for this Country and about 3 inches of snow and ice We have got a new lot of tents What they call Sibly tents they are 15 ft wide on the ground and they are the shape of a bell and there is 14 of us in a tent and we have 3 stoves siting in the center and we are warm and comfortable we cook our own meat and we expect to do all of our cooking in a day or to You wanted to know if Henry Bradshaw father was from the east

Camp Tenton Jan 15 1862

Father
            I am well at present and I hope you and Mother is the same I spose you are looking for me home & but I dont know now when I will come home We got our pay yesterday but we did not hear anything about geting discharge and I begin to think we will have to stay untill the war is ended witch I think will be ended less than 6 months unless England turns in agenst us but I

he says not he always lived in Chautqua Co from your son
                    Nelson Taylor

              Camp Fenton Jan 26th 1862
Father
       I have not sent my money home yet as I exspected to do the reason is because I could not get a pass to go to the City last week but I will get a pass as soon as I can and send it for I dont want it with me They paid us in Treausery notes I supose they are as good as the Gold We are haveing very unpleasant wether hear now it is rainy mudy and snowing a little evry day for over a week and it is march wather cold winds Frezing and thawing. I am well at present and I weight 190 lbs Soldiering agreas with me first rate I am cooking now for our mess we take turns around and do the cooking for a week and we have Pork and Beans for Dinner every day that Account of my wighing so heavy. There has one man deserted from our Company the 3d night after we was paid and there was 4 out of the regtiment that has Deserted since we have been here and they caught too of them before they got to Baltimore and they are a going to court martial them soon The man that Deserted from our Company is over 50 years old and I dont think they will ever find him

Write as often as you can I dont think of any thing more at present from
              Nelson Taylor

Washington Camp Fenton Jan 28th
Father

I thought I would run the risk of sending my money in a letter For I cant get a pass to go to the city to send it by express And you will find $40.00 if you get the letter write as soon as you recieve it and let me know that it went through safe I am well at present from your son
              Nelson Taylor

            Camp Fenton Feb 6
Dear Father

I recieved your letter to day and I was glad to hear you wer well and that you recieved my letter with the money in it I was a little uneasy about it for fear it would not go through You wrote about my being vacinated I was vacinated 2 years ago this winter and it worked good and I was vacinated when I first enlisted but it did not work any for I have a good scar on my arm now. You wrote that you heard they had the Small pox in Col McKeeans Regt it is news to me I saw Peter Simmons about 10 days ago and he did not say any thing about there having the Small Pox We have not had any cases of it in our Regt. There was one man broke out all over and they thought he had the small pox and they took him of to the City hospital and the Docktor said it was the effects of hard drinking and by his brakeing off from it since he has been here You heard there was 2 Cavalry Regtiments disbanded I have not seen anything of it There was a man from the Rebel Army came in to the City of Washington Bearing a flag of truce day before yesterday I heard his buisness was to tell President Lincon if he hung thoes bridge burnere in Missouri they would hang the same number of Union Officers witch they have got as prisoners That is the report here now You wanted to know about when we will be out Col said we would have our horses by the 1st of march I dont think we will get them before spring if we get them at all. We have got a Brass Band for our regtiment now the Officers are to the expense of it. I am well at present from your son

     Nelson Taylor

    Camp Fenton Feb 18
  I will now write you a few lines and let you know that I am well and I hope thes lines will find you the same We got the news here last night that our troops had takeing Fort Donelson and 15,000

prissoners It created quite an excitement
in all of the Camps around us here fireing
of Cannon and musketry for an our or too I
got a letter from Hi and Han they wer well
he has sold out to his father I was out on
a pass a few days ago and I had my Pitcure
takeing and I will send it to you it is
not a very good one but I will send it.
Our Regt will not get any horses or arms
by the way things works now that is my
opinon but there is a goodeal of hard
fighting to do in Virginia yet for some to
do
  from your son
     Nelson Taylor

    Camp Fenton Mar 2
 I am well at present and I hope these
few lines will find you the same You may
not get this untill after the 15 for the
report is that the mail is stoped from
going out of the City and they have stoped
the papers from printing the war news here
till after the 15th of march We were
Mustered for pay the 28 of Feb   We will
get our pay next week Congress has passed
a Bill to reduce the Cavalry forces there
is 78 Regt in all They are going to reduce
them down to 50 Regt. Some of the regt
have got 800 men and some have 1100 They
are going to keep 50 Regt of 1200 men
They are going to have an inspection of

the Officers and men and sift out enought to fill the 50 regt and the remainder will be discharge. Wether they well get enought before they get to our regt or not remains to be told We will know by the lat of aprl.

We have had cold and windy wether here for 10 days last monday the wind blew as hard as I ever saw it all day it blew down houses and trees and it blew down the tents in the camps.

It is snowing here to day and it is a hard place for horses there is 3 regt of Cavalry near us here and the horses have to stand and take it just as it comes I got a letter frsom Louisa Walradt and they wer all well from

Nelson Taylor

On March 8 General Sherman requested 150 volunteers to reinforce the Reserve Artillery. The cavalrymen refused to respond to the request. Nelson discusses this refusal in his next letter of March 10. Some friends of the regiment in Washington counselled against the refusal, and the first battalion of four companies left Camp Fenton on March 10 for the march to Camp Duncan east of the capitol and on to Fairfax Court House. Early on the morning of March 12 the battalion resumed its march to Bailey's Cross Roads. Here the battalion was divided into three detachments for service with the several batteries. Nelson's company was not assigned to artillery service but was ordered to march back to Camp Fenton.

Camp Fenton March 10th

Dear Father

I have a lot of news to write you and I have not much time to write. We are under marching Orders and likely to march at any moment. There is 3 Battalions in our regt and the 1st Battalion was ordered to march this morning and they have gone they are going over the river to force them or scar them in to take up with Cannon they dont want us as Cavalry and the Officers want to keep there position and they are divideing the regt up and send them over the river. But every man that went this morning say they never will go in to any other branch of the servis untill they are discharge from this They cannot make us to take any other kind of arms unless we volentear to do it the 2nd and 3 Batalions they are going to try and make them take muskets and goverments property And I for one will not take any other kind of arms unless I am forced in to it and I will be keeped under arest some time before I will do then And there aint one man in our Company but what is of the same opinion we are agoing to hang together and we are going to be careful and not let them get the start of us if we can help it And if there ever was a mad lot of men it is in this Camp yesterday and to day and we laid it all to our we are agoing to hang together and we are going to be careful and not let them get the start of us if we can help it. And if there ever was a mad lot of men it is in this Camp yesterday and to day and we laid it all to our Officers for they have told us all of the time until lately that they could not transfer us in to any other branch of the servis that we volenteered for and know they say they can detach us from our regt and make us take any other kind of arms for a month or to that is the way they are working to get us fast but they cant come it yet.

officers for they have told us all of the
time until lately that they could not
transfer us in to any other branch of the
servis theat we volunteered for and know
they say they can detach us from our regt
and make us take any other kind of arms
for a month or to that is the way they
are working to get us fast but they cant
come it yet. I have not time to write any
more at present I will write as soon as I
can and let you know how we got along dont
be uneasy about me I will try and do the
best I can from your son
                    N Taylor
I am well at present and hope this will
find you the same.

                    Camp Fenton Mar 14th
Dear Father
      In my last letter I wrote you that we
wer under marching orders and exspecting
to leave here any moment Our 1st Batalion
left us last monday they are at Fairfax in
the Artilery servis They refused to serve
as artilery at first but they had to come
to it They have the power to Detach us
for a month or too if they need us in any
other kind of the servis but they hold the
same organization and belong to the regt
and mustered and payed the same as a
Cavalry

Monday we had orders to march tuesday at 10 ocl with 3 days rations and we had orders to give up our sabers and the next morning tuesday they brought in a lot of Rifles for us we had to take them after a gooddeal of refuseing to do it and we left Camp Fenton at 10 and marched along untill dark and we Camped place caled Baileys Cross Roads and the next morning the Col had orders to march back we marched back and we are here in Camp Fenton yet but I dont know how long we will stay here we have got our Rifles but we have not Drilled any yet with them The reason I dont know we think the Col has done something wrong but it is all suposition we think so because they have not drilled us with them We are oblige to obey the order wether they are wright or not I had a letter from Baker yesterday they wer well he wrote that George had Rented his farm and was agoing to move to the Corners It is some 3 or 4 weeks since I have got a letter from you you may have writen and got miscarried write as soon as you can

          from your son

                  Nelson Taylor

MOVING WITH McCLELLAN'S ARMY

The army moved toward Alexandria to take boats down the Potomac and the bay. One of the batteries had moved to Alexandria about March 15 and had to await transportation for two weeks. Cheney relates that "the river was full of boats of every description loading with troops and army supplies. With the movement of the immense army trains and as a result of a severe storm, the roads and fields, and the camps of the batteries became very muddy and the men in the batteries were for days without dry feet. Their shelter consisted of two ponchos tied together over a pole supported by stakes about thirty inches high and a third poncho fastened over one end. This sheltered three men, each man furnishing a poncho. Its resemblance to a dog kennel gave it the name 'dog tent'. Hay, blankets, and overcoats served for bedding. A tallow candle wired to a stake made a light by which to read and write letters." It's safe to assume that Nelson's lot was similar.

The third battalion of which Nelson was a member, had been given their muskets (to which they had objected so strenuously as he related in his letter of March 14) and were drilled in the manual of arms for an infantry escort to the baggage train of the Artillery Reserve. This is probably the ammunition train referred to in the letter of March 17.

Alexandria March 17

Dear Father

We arrived here yesterday about 4 o'clock and we exspect to leave here in a day or too We are Guarding on Amunition train They are fiting out an expidition of 20 thousand troops to reinforce Burnside We exspect to go along with them to guard the trains you may not here from

me in sometime I will write again as soon as I can good by
>from your son
>Nelson Taylor

          Alexandria March 27
Dear Father
    I recieved your letter in due time and found that you wer well I am well at present. We are here yet but I dont know how long we will stay here or where they will send us. They are shiping Troops frome here all of the time the river is full of boats loaded with Soldiers
There has over 100 thousand been shiped from thiss place since we have been here There was 2 young Negroes came into our Camp last night on horse back about 2 oclock They had ran away from there Master near FairFax about 20 miles from here they have gone on to Washington this morning. Most evry day I see some runing away going north I recieved a letter frome George last week and one of his Vendue Bills he said he was agoing to move to the Corners We are haveing very nice wether here warm and sumer like I saw some Letus in a garden that will soon be large enought to eat I comenced writeing thiss yester day and did not have time to finish it 4 of our Companys are down to the dock to day loading Amunition that we are

guarding and I presume we will go off with it perhaps tomorow I will write again as soon as I can from your son
                    Nelson Taylor
Direct your letter the same as you have Only leave off Camp Fenton We get our mail frome Washington yet

About March 28 Hunt's batteries left Alexandria bound for Fortress Monroe using canal boats, barges, and schooners. Troops were landing as rapidly as possible in the crowded harbor. Cannon, mortars, siege guns, and piles of shells were all about the Fortress.

Nelson relates on April 5 that he had seen the iron clad steamer Monitor. It lay hidden among the boats ready to do battle with the Merrimac. The enemy boat was expected any time to raid Federal shipping. However the expected encounter did not materialize.

                    Hampton Va April 5
Dear Father & Mother
    I am well at present We left Alexandria last Tuesday morning at sunrise and we did not get to Fort Monroe untill Friday noon that was yesterday. The steamer that we came on had too Scooners and 1 barge in tow they wer not acquainted with the river and could not run nights and when we got down to the Bay it was to rought to go out and that stopted us 18 hours and we was geting short of Provisions and the quartermaster went

ashore Bought 6 Hogs and drove them down on the shore and dressed them. We are in Camp now outside of the ruins of Hampton City that the Rebbs Destroyed some 2 months ago and there is nothing left now but a pile of burnt Bricks. It is a hard looking site to look at There is a plenty of Fruit trees left that was not killed and the Peach trees are in blow and some are in full bloom you will find one ore too blossoms in this letter. We are 3 miles frome Fort monro on the road leading to Yorktown and about 14 miles frome Yorktown and they are Fighting there to day they comenced this morning 7 ocl and they are at it yet. it is sundown now we can hear the Cannon quite plain Our troops number over a 100 thousand that are there to day they ough to do something but they may have a hard time to drive them out and they are agoing to Atack Richmond next We are in Col Hunts Artilery reserve Col Hunt is acting as Brigadier Gen of the Artilery Reserve we are guarding the Amunition we will folow in the rear of the main army The 77 New York Col McKeean Regt is one of the Regt that is in the number and perhaps they are in the thickest of the Fight as to that I cannot say. I saw the Monoter the Iron Clad steamer that had a fight with the rebel gun boat Merimack She is a hard looking thing to fight I dont know her length

Corectly she is nearly the shape of an egg split into the long way and her deck is 2 ft above water and when she is fighting they sink her down to the watter edge and in her center there is a Cylinder looks like a Chees box where she caries her guns and when a ball strikes that it will revolve around I could see where the balls struck her It dented it some We have not been Paid since January and I cannot tell how long it will be before we will get it and I am out of money I have only 3 cts left I want you to send me 5 dolars in a letter as soon as you get thiss I belive I have writen enough this time from your son
       Nelson Taylor
Direct your letter to Nelson Taylor
Co I 9 NYSV Cavalry
Washington D.C.
And when they get there they are fowarded on to us where ever we are

  The desolation in the village of Hampton must have been dreadful as his letter comments on nothing left "but a pile of bricks." Other accounts paint the village as once a beautiful mostly brick settlement but when viewed on April 5, nothing was left but chimney stacks and broken walls.

  The journey from Hampton was painfully slow for the roads were filled with troops. One battery had covered only three or four miles when night fell, but then as the road cleared somewhat, the batteries made another seven miles to a field of corn stubble. Men lay down to sleep holding their horses' reins. The steward by lantern-light built a fire and made coffee with water he found in an open ditch! The next day the army advanced to about four miles from Yorktown where it went into camp which was named Camp Winfield Scott.

The ground on which the army encamped was historic soil: it was near the place where General Lafayette had his October 1781 headquarters and where Lord Cornwallis's British Army had surrendered that same month.

All the men in the area had left their farms in the care of slaves with women and children occasionally staying on. All occupied houses were safeguarded. The army provided itself with fence rails for fires; hay and grain were taken for horses and mules; cattle, sheep, hogs, geese, turkeys, and chickens were taken to supplement army rations.

It is recorded that the balloon to which Nelson refers in his April 8 letter was manned by General Fitz John Porter. The wind took it over the enemy lines where it nearly dropped, but a "friendly breeze" brought it back safely.

> Camp Windfield Scott Va April 8
> Dear Father
> Perhaps you have heard before thiss reaches you of the Evacuation of Yorktown by the Rebls last Satterday night Sunday morning Gen Porter went up in a Baloon but he could not see anything of the Enemy in sight It was a lively time around here the news spread like wild fire through the camps The Flying Artilery and Cavalry started in persuit and overtook them or a portion of them about 9 miles from Yorktown about noon and the Battle

comenced We could hear the constant roar of cannon all of the afternoon and night The most of the Army here Advanced Sunday and yesterday monday they wer fighting all day it rained very hard the report is that their is a good many kild and wounded on both sids. We have not any corect statements of the Battle yet nothing more than flying reports Before they left Yorktown they had all maners of Infernal machiens fixed to blow up our troops Thousands of shells and Torpedoes just covered up with sand and the moment you step on them they explode The entrance gate to there Forts are all closed and wires attached to the gates and leading to some of there machiens of destruction There was several of our troops kiled and wounded by them I was out there thiss forenoon there Fortifycations are immence I do not see why they left for my part they left a great many heavy guns and amunition I was sure to step where someone had been before and very light at that I dont get any letters yet I am well at present We exspect to go back to Washington soon some time thiss month from your son

     Nelson Taylor

P.S. I had just finished this letter and was eating my supper as the Mail came in and I got a letter from George the first letter I have had from Clifton Park since

I left Alexandria that was from you Father and that was dated 18 March good many of our letters go down to Burnside the 9 N.Y. Infantry regt is there they are sent wrong from Washington we think

          Camp Winfield Scott April 20, 1862
Dear Father
     I am alive and well yet and perhaps thiss will find you the same we are in camp in the rear of the advance on to York Town I wrote you a letter it is some 2 weeks ago and I have not recieved any frome you I think you have not recieved it I wrote you to send me 5 dolars we have not had any Pay since January and I cant tell how long it will be before we will get any and if you have not sent it send it as soon as you get thiss I exspect we will hear some Fighting soon if we do not see it write soon from your son
                    Nelson Taylor
   Direct your letters
   Nelson Taylor care H J Cowden Co. I. 9. N.Y.S.V. Cavalry Washington D. C. and our letters are sent to our regt wherever it may be

       Camp Winfield Scott near York Town Va
              May 3
Dear Father
     I have not recieved any letter from

you yet we do not get our mail very regular since we have been here I got a letter from Able a few days ago it was 3 weeks a coming he said Seth Higgins Gilbert Clements stayed with him over night and that you wer all well Our Pay master came here yesterday and payed us 2 months If you have not sent any money you need not do it now I would not of sent for any if I had exspected to of been paied so soon   Our Regt is Ordered back to Washington to be mustered out of the Service The Order was issued by the Sectetary of war on the 29 day of march The same day we left Alixandria We would of been back to Washington before thiss but 4 companys are in Col Hunts Artilery and he got the order Countermanded untill after the Battle here and it is hourly exspected to begin After thiss fight we will without doubt get discharge We do not exspect to have any of the fighting to do we dont have any Picket duty to do and we have not done anything towards fortifying We have been guarding Amunition a vesel loaded lying at Shipping point and a part of it was loaded onto wagons yesterday We are close enought to see occasionly a shell burst about ¼ amile in front of us into our Camps There is a goodeal of fireing with the Pickets day and night The Rebbs have

> got a good many negroes armed and in the servis here at York Town And the best shott the Rebbs have made is from a negro he climbs up a Chimbly of a recently burnt house and knocking out a brick for a port hole and he sits there and picks off a good many of our men It is low swampy and wet land and mostly timber and Pine under brush if the army has to ly here a month longer there will nearly as many die with fevear as with Powder and ball There is a great many die with Typhoid Fever write soon as you can from your son Nelson Taylor
>
> Direct your letter the same I am well at present and hopeing thiss will find you the same

The siege of Yorktown lasted four weeks and the cavalry companies carrying muskets were very resentful of having been ordered into a service for which they had not volunteered. They objected to carrying muskets any longer when the Army left Yorktown. When the report of their protests reached General McClellan, he issued a strongly worded order condemning the regiments' conduct and offered them an alternative: enlist in the regular U.S. service with the batteries or be discharged.

Two battalions, of which Nelson's was one, upon hearing the order read, piled their guns in front of their officers' quarters. Soon the two battalions marched to Shipping Point to board a vessel bound for West Point from which they proceeded by boat to White House Landing. When the news of General McClellan's order reached Washington, several congressmen presented the case to Secretary Stanton who immediately on May 14, 1862, issued an order that the men of the 9th NY Cavalry be mustered out of service.

The companies' refusal to follow McClellan's order was their vigorous effort to be treated fairly and used as cavalry, the service for which they had volunteered and had been accepted. After the companies had been finally mounted and equipped as cavalry, the unit distinguished itself by courageous and enthusiastic service.

Yorktown Va May 10

Dear Father

We have just got onboard of a Steamer bound for West Point up the York River and the mail came in a few moments ago and yours of the 6 of May is at hand and $5 dollars with it but the other one dated the 11 of April has not appeared yet we recieved 2 months pay the 2 day of May and I wrote to you as soon as we wer paid to not send any money if you had not But I will take care of it I wont risk any more in letters I comenced thiss letter on the boat and I could not finish it there for there was to many sights to see along the river we had a pleasant trip of 3 hours ride and we arived at Westpoint 1 ocl and there is no landing here and the boats could not come within ¼ of amile of the shore and we had to load our lugage horses and wagons onto boats or what is cald Pontoon Bridges and land in that way and it was dark and after when we landed and

Pitched our tents for the night near the bank of the river we are haveing very warm and pleasant wether here now trees are all leaved out grass and winter Wheat look very nice

    We will leave here for Richmond or some other place to morrow or next day the army that lays here now marches to morrow and we think Richmond is our destination Our Regt may not get away from here in to or 3 day for we will have to get the Amunition Trains ready it is on to a vessel yet When our troops landed here they had quite a battle last monday I think it was they landed You get the News of the war as soon as we do and a little sooner We get New York Papers and the news go there and back before we get them corect Well I must close for it is geting late and I want to write a few lines to hannah tonight good by N. Taylor

                                Westpoint May 17
Dear Father

    I recieved your letter dated the 7 of may day before yesterday and I would of answered it before but we are exspecting to go back to washington now and we will go as soon as we can get a boat to take us and we will be mustered out and Discharge. We are here at westpoint yet We landed here a week ago to day and it is a nice contry all along the river from Yorktown up as far as we are There is some pieces of Winter Wheat knee high and now and then a very fine garden I was in a garden yesterday and there was a bed of straw beries some of them wer ripe the handsomest I ever saw I recieved your letter of may 6 with 5 dolars in it and I wrote one to you as soon as I recieved it. Well I have wrote to you so many times about our being discharge and it has not proved true before but it is a sure thing now for we have orders to that effect and we are waiting for a boat to take us no more at presant from your son Nelson Taylor

    White House landing Va May 20
 I comenced this letter last satterday and not haveing any chance to send thiss out untill to day I thought I would write a few lines more Sunday night we wer ordered to report at Head Quarters as soon as we could to be mustered out we got on to a boat and came up here yesterday and landed thiss morning Our Regt is all together now but one company and they will be here to night We will be mustered out to morrow or next day as soon as the papers are ready Our regt will be transported to Albany before we will be disbanded we will get there some time next

week you need not write any more untill you heare from me again your son Nelson Taylor

Washington DC May 26
Dear Father
In my last letter that I wrote to you we wer at the White House Landing Va and that we wer Orderdered there to be mustered out The day I wrote that Order was Countermanded and Ordered to go to Albany to be Discharged we returned our arms Horses and wagon over to the Govertment and was all ready to take the Boat the next morning About dark that Order was Countermanded and we wer Ordered to Washington to be mounted and It is verry probable that we will get our Horses and other equipments. But when we will get them I cant tell we have Orders one day they Countermand them the next. We are in Barracks out on 7 st good comfortable quarters the best we have had since we have been in the servis Our Capton H J Cowden is Dead he died last Thursday athe White House landing the same day we left there. His remains wer taken to Fortress monro and Embalmed and sent home He was sick a little over 2 weeks with Intesmitis Fever It is reported here that General Banks has been driven back to Harpers Ferry And they are afraid the

enemy is a going or have left Richmond and comeing here to atack Washington I have not time to write any more at present I will write in a day or too again I am well from your son

                        Nelson Taylor

Direct your letters
    Nelson Taylor
    Co I 9 N.Y.S.V.Cavalry Col Beardsly Camp Washington D.C.

                    Washington May 30

Dear Father

    I will now give you a short History of our regt since we left here last spring. You know that we wer Detacth last march and 4 Companys wer sent to Col Hunt Artillery and the remainder of the regt had too take Rifles. We were Detacth for 30 days and then we wer to be Mounted or sent home Well now when the 30 days wer up we wer at Hampton Va and the 4 Companys that wer in the Artillery wer at the Advance at York Town. As soon as the 30 days wer up Secretary Stanton issued an order and sent it to General Wood to have the 9 NYSV Cavalry Paid and Mustered out of the servis It was exspected to have a battle at York Town soon when this order came Col Hunt wanted to keep thees men as long as he could. he goes to Gen McClellan and tells him about the order and that he could not spare the men untill after the Battle. Well then they had the order stayed untill York Town was taken and then the regt would be got together and discharge. When the Rebbs left York town Col Hunts Artillery was the first to give chase and our boys wer with them and then we did not hear any thing from them till after fight at Wiliamsburg. Then they refused or a part of them did to serve there anny longer Well at the same time the rest of our regt we wer at York town yet One company after another said they would never carry there Rifles any farther and some companys went so far as to carry them to there Captons and stacked them in front of there tents and said they would not carry them anny farther at this time 60 days had roled around and they would of kept the regt in the same shape untill the end of the war if they had keept still Our Regt was reported to Gen McClellan as being in a state of mutiny then we wer ordered to West point Some Campanys carried there rifles and some would not I carried mine untill ordered to give it up and so did our Company The next day after we got to West point Gen McClellan sent an Order to our regt and it was read to us and enclosed you will find a coppy It was a general Order and it was read to all of his army at that place Well

after we read the order it looked as if he was a going to drive us into the Artillery or give us an dishonerable discharge We complyed with the order and our names wer sent in as disaffective Then we wer ordered to White House landing his head quarters wer near there at that time. When we got there and got the regt altogether we wer to be mustered out there. Well then he ordered us to go to Albany New York before we wer mustered out we wer all ready to take the Boat last Thursday and then we had a different Order
  Senators Kings, Frank, and Fenton took a conciderable intrest in the regt for it was the only full regt raised in that district They done all they could last winter to have the regt fuly equipt they had quite a number of friends in the regt and the fact of it is the regt has been misused by puting it in the shape that it was And they wer informed of all of it transactions and they say the regt has been used as bad as any regt in the servis and they was informed of this order immediately Well they reported to Secketary Stanton how the regt had been used and then at the last give them a Dishonerable discharge it was useing them to hard Well then he issues an order for the regt to come to Washington for the purpose of being mounted and we are here

now and I think they will equip us as soon as they can we have got our Sabers now same ones that the 9 N.Y had It will be some time before we will get our horses for there is 4 regt to have there horses before ours gets any I recieved a letter from Mary yesterday datted May 16 Well I dont know of any more to write this time give my love to all I am well at present from your son

        Nelson Taylor
Direct N. Taylor c/o 9 N.Y.S.V. Cavalry Col Beardsly Command Washington

    9 N. York Cavalry
Head Quarters Army of the Potomac
 Camp at Ropers Meeting House
   Va May 11th 1862
    General Orders
     No. 121

 It haveing been reported to the Commanding General that the 9 Regtiment New York Cavalry is in a state of disaffection he deems it unjust to the brave soldiers who constitute this army that men thus displaying a spirit of cowardice in face of the enemy should remain longer with them. the Commanding Officer of the regiment will prepare lists of the men thus showing themselves unworthy to belong to this Army and forward the same to there Head Quarters to

the end that these persons may be
discharged and that the army and the
Contry may be made acquainted with the
names of thoes who have basely held back
there servis in the time of there countrys
need These lists will be given to the
army and the public It is to be hoped
that there are many in the regimant who
are animated with the desire to
participate in the battle exspected soon
to take place. Men thus honorably
disposed will be sent by there Colonel to
join the Artillry Reserve where there
servis can be more usefully employed at
this moment than in any other way

By Command of Major General McClellan
        S. Williams
Assistant Adjutant General Official
Aide de Camp

              Washington DC June 16
Dear Father
    I now take the opportunity of
writeing a few lines to you to let you
know that I am well and enjoying good
health at present and hopeing thiss will
find you the same The wether has been
very hot here for a week past untill
yesterday and it changed around cold very
neer cold enought for a frost last night
Yesterdy noon we had Orders to get out of

the Barracks as soon as we could for they wanted to use it for a Hospital they exspected a good many Sick to come in yesterday They took all of the largest Churches in the City yesterday and took the seats out and useing them for the Hospital Well then yesterday we had to pack up and leave the Barracks and go into tents again close by and this afternoon when we had got nicely setteled in our tents we had Orders to go back in the Barracks again It apears they do not want to use the buildings here yet our tents are left standing ready to go into witch I think we will have to before a great while for there is a great many sick a comeing in from the Army of the Potomack. We wer payed 2 months Pay Satterday again

    We have not got any Horses yet we exspect to have some of them this week This is the greatest place for Straw Berrys that I ever saw It is a show to go in the Market mornings and see the Strawberrys as well as everthing else in the Vegtable line. We can get them for 3 cts a quart and the very best for 5 and 6 cts Write as soon as you can from your son   Nelson Taylor

Direct Nelson Taylor
 care A. M Corigan Co I 9 N.Y.S.V. Cavalry Washington D.C.

As soon as the Cavalry was mounted and fully equipped, the camp life and routine changed greatly. Cheney graphically describes the camp life and drill, and it is quoted here verbatim:

"On June 21, Hon. Preston King, Mr. Fenton and Mr. Frank again called on the Secretary of War and were told by Mr. Stanton that he had 'made up his mind to mount the regiment.' The last of June horses and equipments were received nearly sufficient to mount all the men fit for duty. On July 1, the regiment marched to Cloud's Mills three miles from Alexandria toward Fairfax Court House and about nine miles from Washington where it joined Gen. Sturges' Brigade. There being many more horses than saddles and bridles, many of the men rode bareback with only a rope to guide their horses. The effects of that ride were deeply felt for many days. A number of men, not yet mounted, marched on foot or rode in the regimental wagons. In a few days enough horses and equipments were received to mount all the men. Camp duty and drill were now entered upon with much interest and enthusiasm. The order of camp duties was about as follows: The first thing heard in the morning was the chief bugler near regimental headquarters, blowing the call, "Assembly of buglers," when all the company buglers assembled at the tent of the chief bugler and they blew "Reveille" at 5 a.m. Each company then formed in two ranks on its company street and the First Sergeant called the roll. Then came the bugle call "Stables" and the First Sergeants gave the order "get your feed." The men then proceeded to feed their horses which were tied to long cables stretched along the company streets. Oats were dished out into the nosebags by the Quartermaster Sergeant. Then came the order, "groom your horses." After grooming the men washed and got breakfast. Then the bugles blew "Water call," and the order came "bridle up," "lead out" and the men mounted their horses without saddles and rode to water under command of a sergeant or lieutenant. Then the bugles blew "Sick call" when the sick, which included all who wished to be excused from duty, were marched to the Surgeon's tent. About 8:30 a.m. the bugles blew "Guard mounting" and the First Sergeants gave the order "Guard saddle up," "Lead out," "mount," and a sergeant marched the men to the color line. The guard consisted of five or six men from each company who had been previously notified and they were posted around the camp of the regiment. After guard mounting came company drill when the First Sergeants gave the orders "saddle up," "lead out," and after forming the company turned it over to the captain saying, "Sir, the company is formed." The Captain then gave the orders, "prepare to mount," "mount" "form ranks," and marched the company to the drill ground where an hour or two was given to the evolutions of the trooper mounted. Drill was conducted both forenoon and afternoon. Dress parade was held at 6:30 p.m. So the men were busy every day and there was heard bugle calls, orders, drill, dress parade, some grumbling, some sport, not forgetting to eat three times per day and some of the men not forgetting to drink at odd hours something stronger than coffee if they could smuggle it into camp.

"The following 'Synopsis of Camp Life of 9th N.Y.Cavalry, copy submitted by Corporal Wilson, Co. K.'gives an interesting interpretation of the bugle calls:

 At sunrise, Reveille. Fall in for Roll Call.
 6 a.m. Stable call. Feed and Groom your Horses.
 7 a.m. Breakfast call. Pork, Hardtack and Coffee.
 7:30 a.m. Water call. Water your horses and feed some hay.

7:45 a.m. Sick call. Come and get your Quinine.
8 a.m. Guard mounting. 2 Hours on and 4 hours off.
9 a.m. Company Drill. One and a half hours.
9:30 a.m. Fatigue call. Clean Camp and Company streets.
1 p.m. Dinner call. Potatoes, Beans, Pork, Tack and Coffee.
3 p.m. Battalion drill. One hour.
4:30 p.m. 1st Call for Parade. Fall in for Dress Parade.
5 p. m. Dress Parade. Half to one hour.
6 p.m,. Water call. Soon as Dress Parade is over.
6:15 p.m. Stable call. Feed and Groom your Horses.
6:30 p.m. Supper call, Pork, Hardtack and Coffee.
8:30 p.m. Tattoo. Get to your Quarters.
9 p.m. Roll call, and soon after comes Taps, or Lights out. Go to sleep.
Subject to variations according to orders.

Washington D.C. June 23

Dear Father

It is very near a week since I have writen to you I am not very well to day I have had the Diarreia for a few days past It is nearly checked now The wether is verry hot here at present and very sickly. We are in our tents now again we had to move out of the Barracks and they will be used for a Hospital. We do not get any Horses yet and I can not tell when we will we may get some of them thiss week and it may be 2 or 3 months before we get any I had a letter from Han Satterday She wrote that she had been away 3 weeks to Clifton Park while there Mother and Mary went with her to Brooklyn to see Lant she had a boy

Tuesday June 24

As I did not finish writing this Yesterday I am trying to do it now my Direereia was a little worse thiss morning and the Doctor gave me som medcin witch makes me feel worse than I did before and I have no apetite to eat witch of corse makes me very weak but then I am not so sick as to keep my bed I do not think of anything more at present I will write soon again from your son

N. Taylor

Washington D C June 27

Dear Father

I will try and write a few lines to you I am quite sick Thretened with a fever I am only able to sit up for a few moments at a time to day I will go in to the Hospital to day or to morrow Ill get somebody to write for me often your son

N. Taylor

HOSPITALIZED WITH TYPHOID
JUNE 29 - JULY 31, 1862

Washington D C June 29th 1862

Mr. Taylor

Although it is a pleasure for me to do you and my friend Nelson a favor of this kind. Yet it is with sadness that I do a favor of this kind for I know that a letter from me cannot gladden your hearts as those written with his own hand has been wont to do.

Nelson is quite sick with the fever & it holds to him very fast he is not able to write this morning & at his request I am writing for him. He is in the hospital & will have as good medical care as the Regt affords he has many friends in the company that will see that he has good care. He has a good bed & every nourishment that one wants is furnished. The weather is quite warm & the flies are very thick such things tend to make it unpleasant for the sick.

But our sick are brave men (coward would not be here) & they endure this with the same spirit that they would face or persue the enemy. I will write to you every day as long as he is so sick.

Nelson says write amediately & direct to him as usual.

I am Nelsons friend.

Martin Harmon

Washington D. C. July 1st /62

Mr. Taylor

There is not much change taken place here since yesterday except we have orders to cross the river today. all well men will have to go except a very few in the hospital for waters. the sick for all that I know will stay here and the Dr stay with them. Nelson is about the same as yesterday very sick. I will have to leave here I expect & will not be able to write for Nelson again but one of the clerks in the hospital will he belongs to our co & N is acquainted with him his name is Geo. Stockwell If Nelson should get worse it will be quite necessary or at least very pleasant to have some one come & take care of him but if he should get no worse & soon get better what care he will get would do.

Martin Harmon
Hospital 9th N.Y. Cavalry

Washington July 2, 1862

Shubeal Taylor Esq

Dr Sir

By the request of your Son Nelson who is in the Hospital sick with a Fever. I write you requesting you not to come here to see him which is the wish of your Son He tells me that his friend Harmon wrote you to come down immediatley Nelson is

better than he was yesterday and there is
no doubt but what he will be able to
rejoin his Regiment within two weeks. The
Regiment moved yesterday to Cloud's Mills
Va. and also sec^d 320 horses. If any
thing should happen in the case of your
Son I will inform you.

Direct your letters to Washington DC
in care
Surgeon 9th N.Y. Cav
Park Barracks

      G. B. Stockwell
      Act Hospital Steward

 The following letters of July 6, 8, 10, and 15 were written by George Taylor, Nelson's next older brother. George came from Clifton Park to help care for Nelson.

     Washington July 6th 62

Dear Farther

 I left Albany at 4 oclock. Arived in New York 10 in the evening said with Abel the night took the cars at Jersy City 7 oclock arived in Washington at 6 o clock procedied to the Surgeon General office from there to the Medical Directory to get the list of sick in the Hospital but it being the 4th I could not see any one I renewed the search to the Directory and his name was not reported in the city hospital therefore I had to assertain the where abouts of the 9 N.Y. Cavalry they left 1ˢᵗ of July to Alaxandry I went there and found the Regt 4 miles out on the road to Manassis encampt found Capt. Corigan that Regt has a hospital of there own about 2½ miles out of the city I found Nelson there at 4 oclock comfortible Feaver broken and much better than I expected the sick are better cared for in their owen hospital than in the city hospital have every thing they need for their comfort and good nerces and there is 13 sick in their hospital. I will write again to morrow it very warm I must go to the hospital.

                George Taylor

           George Town July 8, 62

Dear Farther

    Tuesday morning I staid with S. W. Sherman last night I left the Hospital at 6 oclock last night Nelson was quite comfortable the Doct told me yesterday Nelson has the intermiten feaver and he had broken it yesterday he had the simtoms of the Tifoied feaver he could not tell under 2 days how it would deturmin he thought that he could break up the feaver beacause Nelson had a very strong contitution to work on he has been gaining strength verry little for 2 days Nelson wants me to stay with him this week to see how he gets along I caried up some ice and

lemmon yesterday that seemed to help the
boys verry mutch. The weather is very warm
last night we had a very heavy Thunder
storm the air seems to be very different
and pure this morning. last Fryday they
sent to washington about 500 wounded men
from the battle field near Richmond every
day their is from 2 to 400 arives in this
city from Battle field Mc Clellen has
been Reinforced to about 50,000 the week
that has past their is men and weoman
here from all parts of Northern states to
find their sick and wounded sons I can not
discribe the scene anguish and sorrow that
is witnessed in this city about day

    I am well as usual I have not time to
write anny more at presant I must go up to
the Hospital I dont think I shall be home
before next monday or tuesday I shall
wait the result of Nelson case no more
                George Taylor

           Washington July 10 1862
Respected Farther
    I sit down to write a few lines this
morning to let you know how we are getting
along I am as well as usuel and hope these
lines will find you and the family
enjoying the same Nelson is about the
same as yesterday. there seems to be no
change with him. the Doct thinks he will
go through with a course of Tifoied feaver

but not so severe as others because he has strong constitution to work on he has been sick about 4 week since he began to complain with the luseness of his bowels. He sits up when he eats also when I make up his bed evry night and morning a few minunits   The Doct had orders from the Quarter Master last night to remove the Convolence to Alexandria And the sick to some of the General Hospitals and there come 4-4 horse Amulance waggons and 6-4 horse Baggage waggons remove them this morning And the Doct went to the City and mad his Statement to the Adjutent General and he told him to remain where he was untill the men got able to do Duty there fore they will remain here untill all are well enough to ride the Horsis for they have them The boys are all well pleased to stay here for they have a good Doct as good in Army as any in the city Nelson wants me to stay with him untill he gets better if I can I want you to write to me what you think about it and also how Esther and the Girls are It cost me about $2.00 per day down into the city I have been staying to a Dutch Hotell about 20 rods from the Hospital 3 day $1.50 but I cannot eat mutch there I have no appitite to eat at this place I must go where I can eat and have food to relish. I shal go down to the city stop at the Clay Hotell

to night there I eat a harty meal as usuel
Isac Chadsey is a Boarding there They say
there is about 50,000 Troops in and around
Washington and there is more comming evry
day there has been about 50,000 sent down
towards Richmond There will be sent 20 or
30,000 more within a week It is quite cool
and a little rainy this morning. To day I
am agoing up to the President Summer
Residence and the Soulgers Home they say
it is a butiful place no more From your
Son Shubael Taylor George Taylor

                    Washington July 15 1862
Respected Farther
    I take another opportunity of writing
a few lines to you let you know that I am
well and hope these few lines will find
you enjoying the same blefsing Nelson is
better the Feaver seem to leave gradualy
he can sit up a little his appitite begins
to come to him alittle I fetched him a
chicken this morning to have it cooked and
to make him some broath. I have not
receiived no letter from home yet. I
think if Nelson keeps againing I shall be
fom Saturday If I dont come you will
heare from me by Saturday. The buoys are
all gaining in this Hospital No more I
remain your son Shubael Taylor
                    George Taylor

Washington DC July 20

Dear Father

 I supose you are looking for a letter from me to hear how I am I am quite well to day I am on the gain Yesterday morning I dress myself and walked around the room some with a cane This morning I feel a litle Stronger but I am very week yet I weight 184 before I was takeing sick but I dont think I will weight much over 150 come to get up I found that was poor than I thought I was

 Tell George that Isac Chadsey did not come and see me the next day George went home he told me Ike was coming up the next day We wer paid 2 months pay yesterday the paymaster came here to the Hospital and payed us the Regt was payed Friday and had orders to march yesterday amd they left but they did not know where they were agoing and where they are I can not tell until we here from them Send that box along as soon as you can I do not know as you can read half of this from your son
      N. Taylor
I write again in a day or to

Washington D.C. July 21

Dear Father

 I am gaining slowly and have a verry good apetite to eat But my feet are so sore I can hardly walk I gess the medcin

I have taken and the fever has setled in my feet but the Doctor says that it is verry common after a fever to have swolen feet or legs he says the skin is agoing to peel off my feet are swolen some and the balls and toes of my feet are verry near as sore as boils I dont know as I will have a chance to try and get a furlough for my feet is so sore I cannot get around and they are going to break up this Hospital next wednesday or thursday and all that is fit to go to Warington they are agoing to send them there a while untill they can get some Horses from the regt for them to ride out where they are and I do not know but they will send me off with them but I dont think my feet will be well enougt to go but if they are they will send me off Our Regt is at Sperryvill about 40 miles west of Warington and they are out near Gen Seigel Division and we hear they are under his Comand and they are where they will have some work to do and before a great while. I sent down to the Express Office yesterday to se if there was anything there for me but there was not any thing there for me and I exspected as much as could be was something there for me but I was disapointed but it is nothing unusual for a Soldier. I had a letter from Able 2 days ago they wer well I have

not had any letters from home since I
recieved his write as soon as you can
from your son
              N. Taylor

              Washington D.C. July 31
Dear Father
    I am getting along slowly my feet are nearly well so I can walk around a little. but I have got a swelling in under my arm now it has been geting sore for a week back and it is about the size of a wallnut and the sorest thing I ever see worse than a boil. I keep a Poltice on it I think it will break in a day or too I went with the Ambulance to the express Office yesterday and found the box there and brought it up to the Hospital and opened it and found everything all wright and none of the cakes wer broken but the tarts wer crumbeled up some but they are first rate. Wel it is all of it good but I dare not eat but a little at a time. Tell the girls I will write to them as soon as my arm gets well for it tires my arm to much to write to day and to morrow they are a going too send us to Warrington and I have a conciderable to do to day It is all most impossibl to get a Furlow there is 4 boys here in the Hospital that will not be fit for duty in 2 months at the least and the Doctor is a trying to get them one I

cant get one without the Doctor recomends it and he wont do that for I am gaining so fast If I had got one and went home it would be only for a short time and the comeing away would be worse than if I had not went at all but for all of that I would come if I could of got one but the Doctor said he could not recomend it I do not get any letters yet from you but I know you have writen and they are careless at the Post office and send them to the regt. There was 1.50 Charges on the box and I had no receipt to show where the box was shipt from and I had to take a man along to prove that was my name and tell where it was started from I told them it was started from one of 3 places Watterford, Cohoes, or Troy and then I had to tell what was in it before I got it and we opened it and found it all wright as I told them. We may stay in Warington some time before we can get to the regt and I will write as soon as I can again from your son N. Taylor

ON POPE'S CAMPAIGN

On July 19 the regiment marched to Warrenton arriving on July 21 to join General Pope. He had ordered that "the country through which the army passes must subsist the army." As soon as the cavalry had dismounted and the picket ropes stretched and the mounts secured, the men followed Pope's order in a great hurry. From a field of wheat they fed their horses well. Then they took pigs, chickens, and other livestock to make a welcomed change from their hardtack rations. In his letter of August 3, Nelson calls Warrenton "the only pleasant place I have seen in Virginia and there is the most nice houses in it." The reader will note that in his next letter, Nelson misspells the village calling it "Warington."

Warington August 3^d 62

Dear Father

We left Washington yesterday morning at 7 and we got here at 3 oclock in the afternoon and this is the only pleasant place I have seen in Virginia and there is the most nice houses in it I was in town thiss morning and you would hardly see a citisan and they are all Secesh here We brought to tents with us and as soon as we got our lugage of of the car we put them up and we have all of the Hospital Stores with anny quantity of Blankets and a plenty of provisions that we brought with us It seems nattural to get in to a tent again. We start tomorrow morning for Sperrysvill tomorrow morning 3 Govertment Wagons to take us and Bagage but we do not exspect to find the regt there we see a soldier that came from there Thursday and he said the regt was under marching Orders and wer packing up to start but wether it is so or not I cant tell. We wont get our mail verry often out here the regt has not had there maill but once since they left Alexandria. We have got a bag full of mail here for the regt and we looked it over and I found one from George mailed the same day you sent the box There is a plenty of Black Berrys in thiss Contry the bushes wer black with them along the rail road I am writing in under the Shade trees in a dore yard of a neat little Cotage There will be a plenty of Peaches here in a few weeks I see some of them are geting red I gess I have writen all of the news from your son

N. Taylor

From Warrenton the regiment marched on to Sperryville and reported to General Sigel who commanded an infantry corps.

On the afternoon of August 10 the regiment had arrived with Sigel's corps from Sperryville. On the night of August 11, Stonewall Jackson moved back across the Rapidan River with cavalry following and picking up some stragglers. During the next few days the cavalry was busy patrolling roads, guarding the fords and picketing along the Rapidan and Robertson Rivers. On August 18 the 9th NY relieved the 4th NY Cavalry which for the past three days had been on picket duty along the Rapidan. Across the river were the enemy's pickets. The 9th acted as Pope's Army's rear guard as it moved rapidly back crossing the

Rappahannock where the enemy appeared in large force on the other side.

For several days and nights the 9th was constantly on the move watching the several fords of the Rappahannock. There were sharp skirmishes with the enemy at Freeman's Ford, Fox's Ford, Sulphur Springs, and Waterloo. On August 28 the regiment marched from Sulphur Springs through Warrenton and Gainesville to Thoroughfare Gap. That evening the regiment moved toward Manassas Junction reaching the position of the Federal army on the Bull Run battlefield.

General Lee's army routed the Federal forces at Bull Run, officially known as Second Bull Run, fought August 29-30, 1862. The Rebels referred to the battle as Second Manassas. It was a most severe setback for the Union. Lee's Army of Northern Virginia had fought brilliantly but from some 54,000 men, had lost nearly 9,500. Pope, conclusively beaten, suffered losses of nearly 14,500 men from a force of some 63,000. Sharp rearguard actions enabled the retreating Federal forces to cross Bull Run Stream safely and head for the Washington area.

Nelson's letters of August 10, 11, and 16 relate the conditions he observed and the plight of both the Northern and Southern troops. Pope's Army was within the line of earthworks protecting Washington. This retreat to Washington marked the end of Pope's Campaign.

Each of the companies of the 9th NY Cavalry had been reduced by the battle casualties to an average of 18 men and horses present for duty.

Culpepper Va Aug 10

Dear Father

We wer at Sperryville when last I wrote you and Friday night about 9 oclock our Division was Ordered to thiss place and be ready to march in an hour. Our regt was the last thing to leave we wer the rear guard. I got readdy and went with them I could stayed there but I would rather come than to stay there and they could not go verry fast and it was 11 oclock Friday night we got into our sadles and startted in the rear and we had to go verry slow a good manny bridges that was not safe and they had to be fit before the Artilery could cross and we marched till after sun rise and we halted and took our breakfast of coffee and hard tack and we got here to Culpepper at sundown and we stoped exspecting to stay all night and it was but a few moments before we wer ordered to be ready to march in 1 hour out to the front & the Capt said I need not go anny farther for it would not be prudent and there was 8 of us left here some not very well and some there Horses was lame. Yesterday they wer Fighting all day out 5 miles from here heavey losses on both sids I had a talk with some of the wounded this morning and one man told me that only 5 men came into camp last night it was one of the Ohio regts they chardge on to a Rebel baterey and the rebles had 3 or 4 regt of Infantry hid in the woods and they mowed them down and took them prisoners and to day it is exspected to have a heavey battle to day but it has been verry quiet all of the morning our Company quartermaster came frome the regt thiss morning and he said they never took there sadles off last night and they had been on since Friday night 9 oclock but the boys got some sleep last night but on our march out here when ever we would dismount the boys would lay down and be asleep in a moment. It is all quiet out to the front yet and it is reported here that Jackson has moved around and are trying to flank us on our rigt flank we will stay here day or too before we go to the regt. Our teams are back a mile from here loaded forage and they have got our tents and tents are of no use only when it is rainny for the boys spread there blankets on the ground and lay down and sleep it is verry hot and dry here and dusty.

Monday morning Aug 11 I will write a few more lines this morning our Doctor came here a few moments ago from the regt and he says the wounded numbers a little over 1,000 of what they have got off of the Battle field and the Dead all lays on the Battle field yet the Battle field lies between the to armys and they are only 1/8 mile apart and the dead of both army lie there on the field yet and no doubt but there is a good many wounded there to suffering and they cannot get to them to take them off they dont know how many are kild there was no fighting our regt was out all day yesterday reconoitering they went around and got in the rear of the army in the left rear. they exspect to have a Battle again to day Jackson and Pope will get cleaned out now before a great while I think Pope will whip him our regt has not had any fight yet but they will have some to do soon. We are liveing first rate here now there is 8 of us here together we have to forage our own feed for our Horses we are now out of wheat and we feed that 2 of the boys went out thiss morning and brought in a pig and took hiss hide of and we had fresh Porkfor Breakfast and 3 more of the boys went off and brought back there canteens and cups full of milk and once in while we get a mess of new potatoes and green corn I am gaining slowly but I am not strong enought to stand the work the boys have to do now they are in the saddle the most of the time and we will stay here 2 or 3 day yet and perhaps longer I write soon again from your son Nelson Taylor

Aug 16th 1862

Dear Father

When I wrote you last I was at Culpepper. I am with the regt now doing

duty I am well and have a good apetite
The day that I wrote to you before our
Wagon train came up where we wer and they
wer a going on to the regt and we went
with them and it was too days before we
over took the regt we passed over the
Battle field and I went all over the field
but it is all most impossible for a person
to pass it for the dead Horses. The Enemy
went of without burrying all of there dead
they left Tuesday night and our troops
buryed them Wednesday. They left them 6
or 8 in a pile they found a number of
piles of them and what they did bury or a
good many of them they covered them up
where they fell arms or legs sticking out
and some 8 or 10 piled up together and a
little dirt throwed onto them it was the
most horrorable sight I ever saw. We got
to the regt Thursday night a little before
sundown and about 12 our Company and
Company H was ordered to saddle up be
ready to march in ½ hour. I went with them
we went out on Picket we wer out to the
Rapadian River and railroad is the line
between us and enemy. Rapadian Station is
where we wer ordered to go. The rebles
pickets are on the other side of the river
in sight of us all day they are going to
make another stand there i think we
stayed there till dark and then we wer
relieved and then we came back to camp

PLATE VI

A CAVALRY CHARGE

they keep the Cavalry a going nearly all of the time on picket and scouting we have to keep our things readdy to throw on our horses in a moment warning we have no tents when we sleep we use our saddle for a pillow and the blue sky for a roof if it rains we strech our blanket over a pole We are liveing well now a plenty Green corn new potatoes fresh meat of all kinds Peaches are geting ripe some of them When we are out we take every thing that we want to eat for our selves and Horses and our army strips every thing clean. I have not time to write anny more at present I just recieved a letter from ester and she said father had writen 2 letters but I have not had but one letter before since I left Washington and that was from George I will write as soon as I can again from your son   Nelson Taylor

Tell Ester to write as often as she can and all the rest I wont have time to write as much as I have and I will write to Father as often as posible and George and John's Famlys can read it the same as if it was sent to them.

DEFENDING WASHINGTON

The hardships of the service had been so severe that the companies of the 9th N.Y. Cavalry had been reduced to an average of 18 men and horses available for duty. On September 3 the regiment marched to Hall's Farm where men and horses took well-deserved and needed rest. A large number of recruits and fresh horses and equipment were received. Nelson's letter of September 17, 1962 was written from Hall's Farm.

Lee's army, advancing into Maryland, was defeated at the battle of Antietam on September 16 and 17. The 9th Cavalry remained with Sigel's corps in front of Washington and did extensive picket and patrol duty. The pickets were gradually advanced from Falls Church to Vienna, Hunter's Mill, Thornton, and Herndon Stations on the railroad toward Leesburg; to Fairfax Station, Union Mills, and Manassas Junction on the Orange and Alexandria railroad; and to Chantilly, Centerville, Gum Springs, and Bull Run on wagon roads.

Nelson's letters of September 25, 28, October 8, 10, and November 9 were written from the Centerville area.

Arlington Heights Sept

Dear Father

It is some time since you have heard from me and the reason is I have not had time before in to weeks except one afternoon and then I wrote one and could not send it off You have no doubt heard of our army falling back to washington or its vicinity too weeks ago monday we left the Rapadan river and we did not take the saddles off of our horses but too nights in the time we see soldiering in full I have seen 4 Battles in the time 2 on the Rapahanock river 1 at the Sulphur springs and the fight at Manasa our regt has not done any fighting yet but we have under fire at all of the fights I have not time to write all of the partickulars now I am well and stood the march much better than I exspected night and day has been all the same we wer on the go all of the time nearly over fences ditches stonewalls wood rocks mountains and I dont know what not balls and shells flying around our heads I used up one horse the first ten days and I hapened to find one running loose the same day and he is a good one we are 7 miles up the river from Washington on the oposite side of the river dont know how long we will stay around hear some talk of our going to Harpers ferry our horses are saddled and ready to move to some place what sleep we got we would tie the Bridle reins to our arms or legs and lay down by our horses heads I do not know as you will get this in some time there has no mail been sent from our army in too weeks the mail has been stoped for some cause and if I have a chance to send it to washington I will do so I have not had any letters from you yet we have not had any mail for 2 weeks write soon from your son   Nelson Taylor

Camp on Halls farm across the river from Georgetown D.C. Sept 17

Dear Father

It is over a week since I have writen to you I recieved a letter from Hi and Han a few days ago saying that you wer all well as usual We have moved our Camp since I wrote to you we are about 3 miles from Georgetown on the Va side We are not doeing much of anything at presant only geting our Horses Shod up ready for a march and doing Picket duty we are on Picket about once a week we wer posted on the Leesburgh turnpike 1 mile beyond Falls Church and nearly 6 miles from Camp We have high liveing when we are out on picket we get all of the Peaches and other fruit we want and thiss is a great place for grapes some of the best I ever eat they appear to grow wild where there is a brook and low wet land in the woods there is a plenty of them We had orders yesterday to hold ourselves in readiness to march at a moments notice but in what direction we will go I cannot say I am well at presant and hopeing thiss will find you the same write soon from your son

Nelson Taylor

Centerville Va Sept 25th 1862

Dear Father

As we have moved our camp again I

thought I would write to you and let you know where I was and what I was a doing. We came out here Sunday night and a part of our Division is out here We are doing Picket duty every other day since we have been out here and I am on picket to day we usualy have from 3 to 10 on a post our lines are out as far as bull run battle field there is some of the enemy Cavalry seen most every day on the other side of bull run we think they have some troops out near Warrenton but how many do not know

Sept 28th
    Sunday

I commenced writeing thiss 3 days ago and I have not had time to finish it since when we are not on picket we are out a scouting and what time we are in camp we improve it well by cooking eateing and sleeping each man draws his rations for 2 or 3 days and cooks it to suit him self and it matters not where we are we have our Bed and board on our horse with us A part of our regt went out reconoitering yesterday we went out far as Gainsville and New Market 2 Rail road Stations on the Warrenton and manassa R road. We saw a few rebs at the latter place but they left as soon as they saw us we took one prisoner at new market we think he is a spy and 3 at Gainesvill and they wer wounded soldiers and our Major Paroled them and left them and it was 12 oclock last night when we came in camp and thiss morning 2 companys of us wer sent off with a train over to Manassa station to guard the train the wagons went over after horse shoes and other iron where the rebs burnt so many cars for us they destroyed about 200,000 dolars worth of property for us.

When I came back I found a letter here for me and found it was from mary and that you wer all well except Ester I thought I would answer it with thiss it is most dark and the mail goes out early in the morning and ill have to finish it to night for we may 10 or 20 miles from thiss place before morning.
Mary you wished to know wether our letter wer inspected or not they are not unless they are broken open after they leave us we have the privalige of writeing what we please as far as I know and about the war comeing to a close it does not look much more like it know than it did a year ago and it is a matter of question witch side will whipp There is a good many wounded around here with the inhabtants reble Soldiers and they say they will never give up that is the south as long as there is a man left they say they will have there one way or die a trying Tell Mother I will

> *send her some grape seeds when I find some*
> *again fruit of all kinds is striped here*
> *now by the soldiers I will write again as*
> *soon as I can I am well at presant from*
> *N. Taylor*

On October 1, following a report that a large Confederate force had come through Snicker's Gap, the 9th NY along with the 1st Maryland Cavalry were sent out to reconnoiter. The enemy's pickets were found at Aldie, but no large force was east of the mountains. On October 13 a battery and four regiments of cavalry including the 9th NY left Centerville at 2 a.m. in a drizzling rain and marched to Aldie fifteen miles away arriving at daybreak. Patrols were sent out on the several roads, one detachment going toward Leesburg and a portion of the 9th to Middleburg.

About October 10 the 9th rode to Aldie where it captured forty men, an ambulance, and two wagons loaded with provisions. The prisoners were paroled.

October 16 a large part of the regiment made a reconnaissance of three days beyond Thoroughfare Gap. On the night of October 23 a report came in that some of the cavalry pickets had been driven in and some of the infantry pickets captured. Orders came for some of the companies to saddle up and report to General Stahl in fifteen minutes. These companies rode with the General to Chantilly, four miles north of Centerville on the Winchester Turnpike. Chantilly was the magnificent country residence of Lee's greatest cavalry leader, General J.E.B. Stuart. The place was now occupied by the Union troops.

> *Centerville Va Oct 8th*
> *Cos Mary*
> *As I am not well enought for duty at present I have time to write you a letter*

in answer to the one I recieved from you a short time ago. I have had the Dierriea for a day or too and am not quite rid of them yet. We are haveing verry hot and dry wether here and the water is not of the best quality witch we have to use You wanted to know how I like our Officers I like them well enought. We have no Comishaned Officer withe the Company now Our Capt is with Col Beardsly. Col is Acting as Brigadier Gen of our Cavalry Brigade and our Capt is one of his staff our first Lieut is home recruitting for the regt and has been for 2 months or more our 2nd lieut is home on a furlough sick Our Orderly Sergent he is sick at Washaington and 2nd Sergent Burroughs has Comand of the Company. We have only 30 mounted men in the Company nearly as many Dismounted. We have 200 new recruits for the regt and about the same number of old soldiers without horses there horses are worn out we are exspecting a suply of horses soon The army is not doeing mutch of anything here only fiting up for a fall Campaign we may remain here for some time. Before we came out here they give Carbiens and we are as well armed as any regt in the servis now and we drew Rubber Ponchoes or Blankets and they are just the thing for a wet day.

Centerville Oct 10

I comenced thiss letter the 8 and before I finished it we had orders to pack up for a march and we remained readdy untill night and we then had orders to unsaddle and we are campted here yet. Our regt went out the same day in the direction of Leesburgh as far as Alldee and they captured from the Rebs 2 Waggons loaded with Bacon 4 mules on one waggon 4 horses on the other and 4 prisoners and brought them in to camp with them and the next morning they wer sent to Gen Segel Head Quarters at Fairfax Court house. We had a share of the Bacon before sending it off Gen Sigl is reviewing his troops here to day ansswer this as soon as you can from

N. Taylor

Centerville Va Nov 9th 62

Dear Father

I wrote a letter to George a few days ago saying we wer under marching orders and exspecting to go back near washington to recruit up but instead of that Seigl Corps has made an Advance and our regt with the rest that had horses fit to go about half of our horses are sick some with the Distemper and some with the Black Tonge and new deasseas there tonge will be a raw sore and go 4 or 5 days with out

eating my horse had the sore tonge and I did not go all of the servisable troops have moved they are out the whole Army is makeing an Advance. We have just got Orders to move camp but in what direction I dont know We have had 4 or 5 days of very cold wether for thiss contry and it snowed yesterday verry hard all day and the boys on the advanc have had a hard time of it but the wether is quite pleasant to day. We did not mind the storm much for we have got a comfortable little shanty 7 by 7 walled up with timber 3 ft high we are camped in the woods and have a plenty of wood and we used our ponchoes for the roof and a fireplace in one corner if they will leave us in one place any length of time we can make our selfs comfortable for we have soldiered it long enought to know how to do it. When you write again send me 2 or 3 Postage stamps for it is hard geting them here I have been promoted to a Corporal a few days ago I dont know of anything more to write at presant. I am well write soon from your son
Nelson Taylor

Shantila farm Va Nov 23rd 1862
Dear Father
It is so long since I have had a letter from anny one I would hardly know

how to read one if I did get one. We moved camp from Centerville week ago friday out to Aldie and we stayed there untill monday and then we moved to Hopeville Gap. Siegel troops wer stationed at Aldie Hopeville gap Thouroughfare gap and gainsville and when Burnside advanced Siegel was left for the Reserve corps and he has moved back to Fairfax and Centervile in order to get forage more readly. We are camped on the Shantila farm 3 miles north of Centervile. We are haveing rather cold windy wet wether here at present to cold to day to write much of a letter I am well at present write soon from your son Nelson

FREDERICKSBURG

The 9th N.Y. Cavalry left Chantilly on December 12 and marched toward Fredericksburg. On Sunday, the 14th, the regiment moved to a spot about four miles from Fredericksburg staying there three or four days. They then moved to Stafford C. H. and encamped in a grove of woods which provided good shelter for winter camps. The following days were occupied with camp and picket duties. On December 27, the pickets were relieved and joined their regiment at Garrisonville. On the 16th of January, 1863, the regiment was ordered to cook three days' rations. This puzzled the men for they had nothing but hardtack so they wondered what to cook.

On January 20 Burnside moved against Lee intending to cross the Rappahannock. The plans were thwarted however, by a series of rain, sleet, and snow storms which turned the roads into a morass of mud. The trains of pontoons and supplies and the army were hopelessly mired, so the infantry were ordered back to camp. The cavalry left camp near the Stafford C.H. and marched to Spotted Tavern or Alcock. On the 21st, the regiment rode to the wagons for hay since they were unable to reach the regiment through the mud and the mired army trains. Cheney reports that a severe snow storm on January 28 deposited a foot of snow on top of six to twelve inches of mud.

In early February the regiment was ordered to be ready to move momentarily to Stafford C.H. This they did on February 10. Supplies brought in by wagons were limited to rations for the men, but there were none for the horses. Even though foraging was constant, there was insufficient feed for the horses. Many animals died from the severe service and lack of feed.

General Hooker had taken command of the Army of the Potomac on January 26, and he immediately reorganized the cavalry service, which up to this time had been attached in brigades and regiments to the infantry corps. They had been unable to adequately resist Stuart's better organized troopers who had easily raided around the army. Hooker organized the cavalry into a corps of ten thousand or more with General Stoneman in command. The regiment moved camp several times and finally settled down at Pleasanton's Landing.

Staford Court House Va Dec 19

Dear Father

I recieved your letter day before we left Chantily and I have not had time to answer it untill now. We left Chantily week ago tuesday and we have been on the move all of the time since. We wer 8 days comeing through the roads are very bad mud knee deep. We went to Falmouth thiss side of the river and about 2 miles from Fredricksburgh and then we wer ordered back here to thiss place Seigels Corps is here we are 10 miles from Fredricksburgh but how long we will remain I dont know. Burnside ocupied Fredricksburgh 2 days in crossing the river and the fight over the other side of the river he lost 15 thousand kild wounded and mising that is the report that we have here. Burnsides army lays thiss side of the river now. We have had rather cold wether for 2 weeks. 2 snow storms in the time. You wanted to know if we drew pay and Clothing enought We can get all of the Clothing we want and at most any time when we are in camp. They payed us 4 month we have enought to eat drink and wear I am well at present from your son N. Taylor

Stafford C.H. Va Jan 2nd1863

Cosen Mary

I recieved your letter last night witch was writen on Christmas and I got it on New Years and I was glad to learn that you wer well as you are I am well at presant and hope thiss will find you the same. We have had a poor Christmas and New Years here in the army nothing only what goverment gave us and no chance to buy anything most all of our Sutlers have been Captured by the rebs on the way from Washington here and that has scared the rest from coming down here. you wondered how we manage to get along this cold wether here is very diferent to what it is up there if it was not we could not stand it we have rather cold nights freese ice ½ inch thick after the sun gets up it is warm and pleasant unless it is Cloudy we have a few days and nights quite cold and then it will be warm and pleasant for a spell we are camped in the woods and we build a little hut of poles and mud and cover it with our shelter tents and build a fireplace in one end so we are comfortable it is a show to go around through the camps and see what style of

PLATE VII

WINTER CAMP

huts and shantys they get up. We heard thiss morning that Burnside army wer about moveing soon but in what direction I cant say. If he moves we will move to I think if we lay here any length of time I will get a pass to go and see Thedore Salsbury he is not more than 10 miles from here You wanted to know if there is any prospects of peace there is sorts of reports in camp but reliable most of the Soldiers have come to the conclusion that this war cannot be settled by fighting but how or when it will be settled is more than I can tell. When you write again send me some more postage samps for it is dificult to get them most of the boys have them sent from home and some sell them as high as 3 for a quarter and they will pay that for the sake of geting them I do not think of any more to write at present from
         Nelson Taylor

     Staford Church Feb 20th 63
Dear Father
  It is sometime since I have writen to you but the reason is we have been moveing around and stormy cold and wet wether and rather poor quarters and not much chance for writeing. we are 3 miles from Staford C.H. and near our old camp which we ocupied when we first came out here. We exspect to move again in a day or too but

where I dont know. They are makeing diferent arangements with the Cavalry here Breaking up our Brigade and puting it in other Brigades and we do not know where we will go yet Gen Stoneman has comand of all the Cavalry of the Army of the Potomac I have not got that Box yet and I dont know when I will get it there is a lot of exspress Boxes in Washington for the regt and as soon as we get settled again if we ever do we may get them I am well at presant and hope thiss will find you the same. from your son

     N.Taylor

   Pleasantons Landing Mar 10

Dear Father

 As it is a stormmy day and not haveing much to do I thought I could not busy myself with anything better than to write a letter home to let you know that I am alive and well but not very comfortable quarters for a wet day only our Shelter tents. The long look for box I got yesterday safe and sound and nearly as good as it was when it started exsept a few of the Apples wer affected and part of the bisket wer molded the cake was all good and so was the dried fruit Butter Sausuage Beef Tea and Tobaco all is good and could not be any better and the fruit is what I think the most of Mother wanted to know if I keept the Teas Spoon yet that she sent me last summer yes mother I have got it yet and intend to keep it as long as I can and I have something else that you gave me when I left home which is worth a great deal more to me and that is the Testament although it is soild some I find great comfort in reading it and if my life is spared to come home I want to bring it home with me

I found George Ushers present in the box and if I had anything to send him I would do it. We are camped here at the landing and will remain here some time untill we get some more horses and the roads dry up We are not alowed wagons any more to haul our suplys but we have one Pack Mule to every 10 men to carry our suplys we did have 20 wagons and we are not alowed but 3 to our regt know and they carry our Amunition I do not think of anything more at present from your son

                              N Taylor

        Pleasantons Landing Mar 31
Dear Father
    I have been looking for a letter from home for a long time but do not get anny. I think you have not got the Directions right or else they have been miscarried I am well at present the wether

is verry unpleasant here to day snowing and raining together. We are here at the landing yet and will remain here untill the army moves I think witch will not be long About half of our regt are unloading suplys at the landing every day and the remainder working roads untill now they are done 100 men from our regt that had servisable horses and that is all we have in the regt have been detaild for Ordelys and Boddy guard for Gen Slocum. We are going to draw new horses soon and we exspect to have some fighting to do this summer. We have quite comfortable quarters here and a plenty to eat and wear I had a letter from Able Baker a few days ago and they wer all well and he wrote that he had sent me a box of things the same day it was rather unexspected I do not think of anny more at presant write as soon as you can from your son
      Nelson Taylor

Direct Nelson Taylor
Co I Pleasantons Landing 9 Cavalry regt
Acquia Creek Va Pleasantons Division

CHANCELLORSVILLE

On April 12 all of the dismounted men of the regiment were detailed to the landing at Quantico Creek to unload boats. One detail unloaded 500 bales of hay and 1,200 sacks of grain. About eighty mounted men were ordered to carry orders and dispatches and to escort general officers. In carrying out these duties they sometimes encountered the enemy and some were wounded and/or captured.

On April 17 the main body of the regiment moved from Pleasanton's Landing to Stafford C.H. Each company had a mule on which to pack blankets and equipage since they had no horses. A seven mile trek brought them to a dry knoll where they pitched camp. Using what lumber they could find, the men built quarters of various designs. From this encampment many of the men were sent out to dig rifle pits.

General Stoneman, with 13,000 cavalry, had moved to the Rappahannock with instructions to harrass and fight the enemy at every opportunity. Stoneman's efforts, however, were not productive of the results expected. Poor managment may have been a contributing cause, and certainly the bad weather was. On the 16th rain caused the river to rise so rapidly that one division was recalled swimming its horses. A series of April storms raised the level of streams and made the roads so bad that advances were postponed. All the time, the heavy cannonading of the battle of Chancellorsville could be heard at Stafford Court House. On the sixth of May the defeated army was moving back into its old camps.

About May 14 a remount camp was located at Pleasanton's Landing. There were about six hundred men and one thousand horses. Men and worn-out horses were steadily being received and detachments were being sent out as soon as the men could be remounted on fresh horses.

Pleasantons Landing April 11ᵗʰ

Broth Hi and Han

I recieved yours of the 5th and was glad to hear from you and home but I am sorry to learn that Hiram health is not very good I have been looking for a letter sometime and had nearly given up geting anny but yesterday yours and one from George came together and not haveing any duty to do thiss morning I find myself writing a few lines to you and all of the Family. It is warm and pleasant here thiss morning and has been for a week past. We are here at the landing yet unloading Suplys and are likely to be in the same busness all sumer for they cannot get any horses for us it apears at presant and they are useing our regt for a Detail regt and they have our regt scatered all over the army now in squads from 5 to 80 in a place as Ordlys Boddy guards cattle guards Division teamsters Division Ambulance Drivers and I dont no whatnot. There is about 300 of us here in camp and we have very comfortable quarters and not very hard work for it is hard to get a soldier to overwork himself. You wanted to know wether they could keep us anny longer than 3 years or not I have heard a good manny say that pretended to know that they could not keep us anny longer than 3 years and I do no think they

will want us anny longer than that anny how. I got the box that Able sent me it was only 10 days on the way it contained a quantity of Lemmon, Ornges some Dried Beef Herring Smoked Ham Box of Figs some mustered and some Dried Prunes and upon the whole I am liveing most to well for a soldier. I sent by mail thiss morning my Comission of Corporalship I thought it would be worth saveing to look at or to show to my grand children. Tell Father to take care of it for me I do not think of annything more of importance to write at presant I am well and have a good apetite and hope this will find you all in the same condition from your Broth
     Nelson Taylor

    Stafford C.H. Va. April 20th
Dear Father
  We have moved our camp to thiss place since I wrote to you before. And we are employed in a diferent kind of work to what we have ever done before since we have been in the Service. We are diging Rifle pits here and when the army moves we are to hold the place and to keep the rear open and a protection to the rail road. There is nearly 400 of us here all told dismounted men some from all regt in our Brigade. We work 1 day out of 5 and that is only enought fore exersise and for our

health. We are haveing warm and pleasant weather now Peach trees are in full bloom We wer Payed 4 months pay satterday and we had to settle up our Clothing Acount to the first of last January. They alow us 3.50 for a month and I did not use up as much clothing as they alowed me quite they owed me $1.61 cents and they payed it with the 4 months Some of the boys used up all they wer alowed and 1 2 and 3 month pay besides to settle up. We have to settle up our Clothing acount once a year. I have been to Acquia landing to day and bought me a pair of boots it is not very often that I can draw a pair to fit me. I had to pay $8.00 for them and while there I had my Pictture taken and you will find it in this letter if you get it. The army it is exspected to move soon the troops are under marching orders and they are exspecting the order to march every day. I will write again in a few days and I think I will send some money to you. I am well at presant and hope thiss will find you all the same it is nearly dark and I must close from your son write soon Nelson Taylor

   Stafford Court House April 25
Dear Father
  As I have nothing to do this afternoon I thought I would write you a

few lines as I wanted to send some money home. Although thiss is not a verry safe way of sending it but as I cannot do any better I will risk it thiss way You will find $20.00 dollars if you ever get this letter if it is not robed by some one before it reaches you

We are diging rifle pits yet I was out yesterday for the first a few days more will finish them up We think of geting horses ennought to mount our regt soon that appears to be the talk now. We are haveing quite warm wether here but the nights are quite cold yet and upon the whole we are haveing quite comfortable times for Soldiers Cavalryman esspeshly.

I want you to write as soon as you get thiss letter and let me know if it came through safe. I do not think of anything more at present I am well from your son
                    Nelson Taylor

            Stafford Court House Va May 11
Dear Father
        It being sometime since I have writen to you I am improveing thees few moments to let you know that I am well and where I am We have got our horses now we got them yesterday and we are bussy rigging up our

trapps and equipments for a march we will leave here in a few days

Our Cavalry has had a large fight on the Rappahanock a few days ago perhaps you have seen some accounts of it in the papers Our Brigade was in the fight and 5 Companys of our regt wer with them and we hear there is a number of them wounded. We have not heard the particulars of the battle yet. We are going to form our Brigade again. we have got the best lot of horses we have had since we been in the servis. It is very Hot and dry here at presant I have a little more money with me than I want and I send in thiss letter 15 dollars. I dont think of anny thing more to write at presant I will write again soon from
     Nelson Taylor
Direct Nelson Taylor
  Co I 9 N.Y.S.V. Cavalry
  Pleasantons Division
  Army of the Potomac

   Stafford C. House Va May 12th
Sister Han
  I have just recieved your letter and as I am not on duty thiss afternoon I thought I would answer it. I am sorry to learn that Hirams health is no better I am glad to learn that you recieved he letter

PLATE VIII

DAGUERREOTYPE OF CORPORAL TAYLOR

with the money you did not say annything about getting a letter with my Pitchure in it. I sent Father a letter a few days before I sent the money with my Degerartype in it. The wether is verry hot heare at present to hot for anny kind of comfort Fredericksburg and vicinity has been the seen of another terrorable Battle and one of the most desperate fought Battles that thiss army has ever had. Perhaps you know more about it than I do for you have the newspapers all of the time we have not had anny papers for nearly 3 weeks untill a few days ago they let the papers come in again I have seen them that was there in the fight and they all apear to say that the Rebs lost 3 to our 1 in kild wounded and prisoners. The Rebs had there Canteens fild with raw Whiskey and Gunpowder all throught the fight and they new no fear of danger of being killed and they would charge on to our Batterys 15 and 20 deep and the Batterys would cut a swath through them with grap and canster shot. The looss on both sids is heavey I have not seen the Official report but no doubt it will exceed 15 thousand kild wounded and taken prisoners on our side 5 of our regt wer taken prisoners we have one hundred men for Orderlys and boddy guards for Gen. Slocum of the 12 Corps 2 of them wer from

our company. We are getting horses now we got 100 sunday and we exspect to have enought in a few days to mount all of us. You said you did not know who our Col was we have no Colonel now he resigned some 3 months ago and Lieut Col. Wm. Sacket has command of the regt and is a verry good officer and soon will be our Col no doubt. Capt McQuin Corigan is our capt yet he is with us now and he is liked well by the company. There was 2 new york regt left here thiss morning there time is up and they are going to Albany and there be mustered out of the Servic They went off feeling first rate they wer in the battle and lost a good manny men I dont think of anny more to write at presant I am well write soon from your broth
     Nelson Taylor
N.B. the one that writes first send me some P. Stamps

GETTYSBURG CAMPAIGN

Food for his army was one of General Lee's primary worries. He was directed to go into Pennsylvania to find resources. On June 3, 1863, he put his army in motion. General Hooker sent a division to determine if the Rebel Army was still in force below Fredericksburg. Finding this to be true, Hooker sent the cavalry to reconnoiter. On June 8 he sent three divisions of Pleasanton's corps to the Rappahanock. At daylight on June 9 the 8th N.Y. Cavalry charged across a ford and engaged the enemy. The opposing forces brought up reinforcements, and Pleasanton was forced to fall back. The Union casualties were much fewer than those suffered by the Southern troops, and the reconnaissance was considered a success. Lee's army was definitely on its way into the Shenandoah Valley bound for the north. The news of the battle at the ford reached the camp at Stafford C.H. the same day.

Within two or three days following, sufficient horses and equipment arrived to mount all the remaining companies. From June 11 until dawn on July 1 when the Battle of Gettysburg began, the regiment was continually on the move: to Bealton Station; Bristoe Station; Aldie; Centerville; Upperville; Snicker's Gap; Leesburg; Middletown; Mechanicstown; Monterey Springs; and finally Gettysburg on July 1st. On that day, men of the 9th on picket post, observed several Confederate soldiers approaching on the road beyond Willoughby Run. The enemy fired at the pickets who returned the fire. This exchange occurred at about 5:30 a.m. and these shots are believed to be the first fired at the Battle of Gettysburg.

In the early afternoon the 9th NY Cavalry was supporting a battery on Cemetery Hill near the Emmetsburgh road. The skirmish line of the Confederate forces began firing at the line of cavalry. Companies G and I (Nelson's company) dismounted and using their carbines and revolvers charged the enemy and drove them back.

Stafford Court House, Va. May 31st 1863
Cosen Mary

Your kind and welcom letter was recieved last night and thiss morning I find myself writing you a few lines It being Sunday morning and Sunday morning inspection over with Sabbath days are verry differrent here to what they are with you. We have no Churches to go to and it is verry seldom that we have Preaching in our regt. We have no Chaplain in our regt now and then a Chaplain from other regts preaches to us. We are haveing verry hot wether here at presant. I had a letter from Orlando Swartwout of the 115 N.Y. regt a few day ago he is at Hilton Head S.C. he wrote they wer well and 4 of there Company had gone home on a Furlough John Filkins and Peter Butlar wer among them Il tell you what the chances are for geting a Furlough here There is only one Furlough granted to a company at a time for 10 days. It is over 2 months since they comenced giveing Furloughs and the 2nd lot has just got back and there is some 18 or 20 a head of me yet and if they dont get along fastter with them in the future than

they have in the past It is to far ahead to look for a Furlough I would like a Furlough now for 30 days wright well We wer payed 2 months pay thiss week. You wanted to know what we had for Dinners Sundays. Well we have everything good such as Hard Tack Coffee and Pork is the stand by for Soldiers I never was as Fleshey and heavey as I am now It is not high living that makes one heavey I think 200 lbs or near that is my heft I dont think of annything more to write at presant I forgot to say the Postage Stamps wer in the letter from your cosen
                              N. Taylor

                   Westminster Md July 4th 1863
Dear Father
     As it is a long time since I have writen to you I think you must be anxious to heare from me I have not had an opportunity to write or anny way of sending anny mail since we left Stafford Va and I have not much time know only to let you know that I am alive and well although I have had several narrow esscapes. We have had a number of Skirmishes and lost quite a number in our regt Our Division had a hard fight July 1st at Gettysburgh Pa We comenced the fight in the morning with only our Division and a part of the first Corps of

infantry and they wer to much for us and drove us back 2 miles before we got reinforcements and then we held our own the rest of the day and reinforcements kept coming in all night and the fight began early in the morning again Our Division was ordered back to this place where we are now to recruite our horsess a little they have been saddled evry day and nearly evry night for 4 weeks and not mutch grain for them to eat. We are 30 miles from Baltimore on a raill road runing to Baltimore. The hardest Battle of the war is being fought now I have not time to write anny more at present write soon from your son

        Nelson Taylor

     Berlin Md July 16th 1863
Dear Sister

  Your letter of June 28 I recieved the 8 of this month and I have not had time to ansswer it before and I hardly know what to write now I am sorry to hear that Hiram is dead and I truely Sympathyse with your early afflictions and misfortunes but I supose it was the will of him that maketh and ruleth all things that it should be so and we must have our trust in him and all things will come out well hereafter. I wrote a letter to Father the 4 of July we wer at Westminster then we went from there over the South Mountain throught to Boonsbourough and Williamsport and there we had a fight on the 6 of this month and on the morning of the 7 we had to fall back to Boonsborough and our regt was the rear guard and we had a skirmish with the rebs and lost 10 kild wounded and taken prisoners in the regt and the next morning Gen Stuart with Cavalry and some Infantry attacked us and we fought them all day and drove them back 3 miles. We had 3 Divisions of Cavalry Gen Bufords Gregs and Killpatrick. We are in Gen Bufords division and have been since we left Va Gen Pleasanton has comand of all the Cavalry We have had some skirmishing nearly every day since we crossed the Pottomac our regt has lost quite a number our Company has been lucky one man mortaly wounded at Gettysburg and one taken prisoner We are camped near the river 6 miles below Harpers ferry and how long we will stop here I cant say but I think not long for we have a pontoon bridge across the river a few miles below here and I understand troops are crossing now Thiss is the first time we have had a chance to wash and dry a shirt since we left Stafford We have a way of our own drying them wash ourselves and shirt and put it on wet The rebs are acrossed the river into Va they got badly whiped at

PLATE IX

AN ADVANCE OF THE CAVALRY

Gettysburgh and they would of got another if they had stoped thiss side of the river a few days longer they crossed in a hurry and a great manny of them got drowned in fording the river I see they are haveing a great riot in New York about the draft I dont know what thiss war is a coming to the only way I see to end thiss war is for every man to show his collors and fight for them Unnion or Disunion nigars or what not Write soon as conveneance from your Bro

      Nelson Taylor

Direct to Gen. Bufords Division instead of Pleasantons

PLATE X

THE PONTOON BRIDGE

AFTER GETTYSBURG
July - November 1863

On July 27 the Division marched to Rappahannock Station. The Confederates were determined to prevent the Union bridge builders from unloading timber to rebuild the railroad bridge. On the 31st the 9th went on picket at Fox Ford but were soon ordered to return to Rappahannock Station. On August 1 the 9th encountered and engaged the enemy near Brandy Station and Culpepper. On August 3 the brigade moved to Kelly's Ford, then on to Catletts Station on the 15th to observe Lee's cavalry activities. The comment on "bushwhackers" in Nelson's letter of September 3 refers to the practice of the inhabitants of the area firing from cover on small groups of Union soldiers. On the 27th the 9th relieved a Pennsylvania Cavalry unit taking over the picket posts at Falmouth.

On October 4 and 5 the regiment was relieved of picket duty and moved back to Stevensburg, crossing the Rappahannock at Eli's Ford. On the 10th the Division crossed the Rapidan and moved up to Morton's Ford. Meade was forced to fall back from the Rapidan and Pleasanton's Cavalry Corps engaged the enemy covering the retreat. At Brandy Station there was hand-to-hand combat with the Confederate infantry.

In mid November the Division marched to Culpepper. The regiment was relieved of picket duty there and returned to camp doing picket duty west of Culpepper.

Near Rappahanock Station July 30th

Dear Father

As I have an opportunity two write thiss morning I thought it best to improve it I recieved Ables letter last night after comeing in from a reconnicance and was glad to hear from home and that you wer all well. We are neare the Rappahanock river and Lees Army is on the opposite side and I think we will lay here for a while and recruit up a little witch will be very acceptable to us for we have had some hard times since we left Stafford. Some long marches with a good deal of fighting and some times short of rations We went five days on two days rations but we had enought to eat except bread we never go hungry for meat fresh meat espeshly The last 3 meals I had 4 hard tacks but we got a plenty when we got here A good share of our liveing now is Black Berrys there is no end to them the largest and best I ever saw I have whished many a time that some of them wer where Mother could pick them but whishing does not much good if it did thiss war would been ended before thiss. We have had a number of Skirmishes amd some of them quite hot work our company has been verry lucky one mortaly wounded at Gettysburgh Pa and 2 taken prisoner the first day of the fight our Division was engadge in it all day and lost quite heavily we Dismounted and fought there Infantry that was the hardest fighting we have had yet We had a fight at Boonsburough Md. on the 8 and 9 of thiss month Our regt has been verry lucky so far but she may get into some place and

come out badly cut up yet. The Cavalry has been of some use thiss summer for we have got better Generals to manage it than we had last summer There is no other branch of the servis suits me as well as the Cavalry I think I never saw so much rain as we have had for the last month we have not had many nights sleep in dry Blankets for a month past I am well and I dont think I was ever any more tought and hearty as I am now write as often as you can from your son
Nelson Taylor
Direct the same as before when you write again put in a sheet of paper and envelop for you can see by this letter that I am hard up for Stationary

Kellys Ford August 6th 63
Dear Sister Han

Thinking you would like to hear from me again I find myself writeing a few lines to you and thinking perhaps you have heard of the late Cavalry fight witch took place on the 1st August thiss month betwen Gen Buford and Stuart Cavalry Our Division crossed the River at Rappahanock Station about 8 oclk in the morning and it was 10 before we w wer all over and then we advanced along the Rail Road towards Culpepper nearly 3 miles to Brandy Station and there we found a plenty of Stuarts

Cavalry and a light Batterry and the fight opened It was as hot a day as I ever saw They stood and fought there awhile and then they comenced falling back towards Culpepper slowly and we folowing Our regt was in the front and under fire all the time Skirmishing Chargeing and meeting charges with them. We followed them nearly to Culpepper and then there Infantry relieved there Cavalry amd then it was our turn to fall back and there Cavalry and some Infantry folowing hurrying us up for 1 hour untill it was dark and on to the same ground where we found them in the morning. Our loss is light for the amount of fighting we done and the number of men we had only about 200 with the regt that day a good manny of our men are dismounted and gone to Washington after Horses. The loss of our regt is 4 kild 17 Wounded 9 missing 27 Horses Kild and wounded mostly kild Our Division lost 200 Kild Wounded and Missing. 3 of our Company Wounded and 3 horses shot A large number of our men wer overcome with the heat and some I heard died from Sun Stroak. I can say that I am thankful that my life and health has been spared so far but we know not what a day may bring fourth and some time I allmost think death preferable to thiss world of sorrow trouble and affliction. We are

camped at Kellys Ford now for the presant but how long we will remain here I cannot say not long perhaps. Write as soon as you get thiss write often as you can and I will do the same from your Broth
N. Taylor

Catletts Station Sept 3 63

Dear Father
It being some time since I have writen home and the fact is I have not had but a very little time for writeing lately. When I wrote last we wer camped at Kellys ford on the Rappahanock and we moved back to thiss place the next day after I wrote and our Brigade Head Quarters have been here at the Station and we have been scouring the Country over after Bushwhackers through London Valley and over to Leesburgh and south of here through Staford County. We would be out from too to four days at a time. We captured a number of prisoners and horses and had 2 men wounded in the regt one day out near Stafford Store. We wer paid too months pay last week and enclosed you will find ten dollars you can keep an account of what little I do send home. I am well at presant write soon from your son
Nelson Taylor

Falmouth Sept 28th 63

Dear Sister

Thinking you may not of recieved my last letters I thought it best to write you a few lines to inform you where I was and what I was a doeing. Our regt is Picketing along the Rappahanock from United States ford down to Falmouth our Company is at the latter place The 6 New York is picketing above us as far as Elis Ford and the 1st Brigade pickets from there to Jemima ford on the Rapidan makeing in all 25 miles Picketing we are out for 7 days our Brigade Head Quarters are near Culpepper We started out Satterday morning was all day geting here it being nearly 30 miles One week ago thiss morning monday our Division and Kilpatrick Division Started out on an expidition the first day we went out as far as Madson Court House and Camped for the night the next morning our Brigade went off in the direction of Ornge C.H. and the others went on towards Stanardsville We found nothing to stop us untill we came to the Rapidan and the ford was well guarded we had a slight Skirmish but the rebs being to many for us we had to fall back with one Lieut and one man wounded in Company K thoes that went off the other way had quite a fight and lost a little more than they made and the next morning we started back to our camp. We wer payed 2 months pay last Friday we are payed up to the first of Sept. We are haveing very pleasant wether here now. I am well and you would think my apetite was good if you could see me eating Hoe cake and Pork sometimes write soon and let me know wether the letter I sent some money in about the first of thiss month to Father give my love to all from your brother

Nelson Taylor

Steavensburgh Va Oct 7th 1863

Dear Father

I recieved Mary letter last night and as she wrote that she was going off soon I thought it best to Direct to you. I am well with the exception of a slight cold witch 1 caught a few days ago while whashing myself but am nearly over it now It is verry seldom that we have colds the changes of the wether does not have the same effect on us that are out in the wether all of the time as it does to thoes that live in houses. We have become seasoned to all kinds of wether and we get along with Soldiering a great deal easeer now than we did when we first came out We are camped at Steavensburgh 5 miles from Culpepper and nearly the same distance from the Rapidan river. I wrote a letter to Hannah about a week since we wer then on Picket down to Falmouth our regt and the 6 N.Y. wer Picketing from Ellis Ford down to Falmouth on the Rappahanock we wer there 8 days and wer relieved Sunday night and came here Monday our Division is camped here for the presant and we make this our Head Quarters when we are not on picket or Scouting the Cavalry is kept moveing around on the Flanks of the Army to watch the movements of the enemy to see that they do not get a force around in the rear of us and cut off our Suplys and Comunications You wanted to know who I tented with well I tent with the Orderly Sergent his name is Naham P Arnold we have messed together since the Maryland Campaign 2 to 4 of us generaly mess together and we furnish our own cooking utensills we have our Coffee Pot and a small Spider to cook our meat one carries Coffee pot and one Spider. I hardly know what we would do if it was not for our Coffee rations witch is the main spoke in the wheel Capt Corigan is with us in comand of the company our first Lieut George B. Stockwell recently promoted from 2nd Lieut in Company G and was assigned to our Company and while we wer on picket last week at Falmouth he complained of being unwell thursday and he stayed around with us that day and he went into a house close by and he was out the next day and he was taken worse in the edge of the evening and died at 5 oclk Satterday morning. The Doctor said the Deasseas was Congestion of the Lungs His remains wer sent home after being embalmed at Culpepper our 2nd lieut John B. Dinsmore is doeing duty at Dismounted Camp at Alexandria where all of our exchange prisoners and thoes comeing from Hospital are sent to get the arms and equipments before going to there regts our Captain is all of the Officers we have with the Company we like our Capt well we have some good men and some bad men among officers as well as among other Class of people. You need not give your selves anny uneasyness about my likeing my Officers for I can get along with them as well as I can with anny body else The most of the Officers in the regt are to slow and eassy and not strict enought to suit me The wether is geting cooll but fair and pleasant we have had too frost the last week This Contry is the verry pictture of Dessolation where the tracks of the army are visable but a verry few inhabitants left through here and they have but a very little to live on only there little garden and a small patch of corn and a great many have nothing only what they get from the goverment We wer payed 2 months pay about

10 days ago they payed us up to the 1st of Sept and enclosed you will find 15 dolars write as soon as you get thiss and let me know wether it goes through safe I think I have writen a long letter for once I will close and get some supper from your son
N Taylor

Camp Stoneman D.C. Oct 22 '63
Dear Father
It is some time since I have written to you or of geting anny letter frome home and the reassen is because I have not been in one place long enought to write for the last 10 days. When I wrote you last I was with the regt at Steavensburgh Va and we broake Camp there week ago last Satterday morning and the report was that Lees army was Flanking our army. Well all of the unservisable horses wer ordered with the Wagon train and my horse being one of that class I went back with the train and was with it untill Wednesday when I was Captured by a party of Mosbys Gurillias on the road from Brentsvile to Fairfax Station I was following along with the train and one of the wagons broake down and that you know makes a break in the train and it was in a thick piece of woods and short turns in the road and I had not got 40 rods from the waggons before a

Camp Stoneman D.C. Oct

Dear Father

It is some time since I have written to you or of getting anny letters frome home and the reason is because I have not been in one place longe enought to write for the last 10 days. When I wrote you last I was with the regt at Steavensburgh Va and we broake Camp there week ago last Satterday morning and the report was that Lees army was Flanking our army. Well all of the unserviceble horses wer ordered with the Wagon train and my horse being one of that class I went back with the train and was with it untill Wednesday when I was Captured by a party of Mosbys Gurillius on the road from Brentsville to Fairfax Station I was following along with the train and one of the wagons broke down and that you know makes a break in the train and it was in a thick piece of woods and short turns in the road and I had not got 40 rods from the waggons before a party of Guirillas jumped out of the bushes and took me and my horse in the woods and keeped me till after dark and took everything I had except what I had on my back and then let me go and even took 5 dollars of money frome me and then I had to foot it then untill I over took our Division train I was to days before I found where it was at fairfax C.H. and where I fund a number of our regt there with played out horses and some Dismounted and over 8 hundred of our Division there in the same condition and we

party of Gurillias jumped out of the bushes and took me and my horse in the woods and keeped me till after dark and took everything I had except what I had on my back and then let me go and even took 5 dollars of money frome me and then I had to foot it then untill I over took our Division train I was to days before I found where it was at Fairfax C.H. and where I found a number of our regt there with played out horses and some Dismounted and over 8 hundred of our Division there in the same condition and we wer ordered to Washington and here we are at the Dismounted Camp 4 miles below the City the Dismounted Camp was on the other sid of the river near Alixandra and they have moved over here lately We are going back to the regt again in a few days they have horses and equipments here ready for us Our regt was badly cut up week ago last Sunday at Brandy Station they loost 60 men in a charge they made there kild wounded and missing 3 of our company wounded and came out and 2 missing and 1 suposed to be dead Our Cavalry has lost heavily in the late movements of the army in men and horses I am well at present Direct your letter the same for I will be with the regt in a few days from your son
      N. Taylor

PLATE XI

THE SUPPLY TRAIN

Near Culpeper Nov 11ᵗʰ 1863

Dear Father

When I last wrote to you I was at the dismounted camp Washington DC and I left there first day of this month and joined the regt again near Bealton Station and we have been on the move nearly all of the time since or I would of writen before. I wrote a letter to John since I came back I found 3 letters here for me one from John 1 from Able and one from Ester and Emma and have not had an opportunity of answering them all yet You have heard before thiss of the forward movement of our Army and of Mead atacking Lee on the Rappahanock and it took Lee so by suprise that he made no stand at all as you may say Mead captured 11 pieces of Artillery and 2,600 prisoners without much loos of life on ether side. Our Division of Cavalry was on the right Flank up to Sulphur Springs and at Jefferson the first Brigade of our Division had a Skirmish near Hasele run on Sunday our Brigade being in Reserve we had no fighting to do Lee Army has fallen back across the Rapidan again. We are Saddle and readdy to move in some direction and waiting for the Orders to march I am well at presant and hoping thiss will find you all in the same condition from your son

Nelson Taylor

Camp near Culpeper Nov 20

Dear Father
      As we are haveing a few days rest in camp I thought if best to write you a few lines to let you know that I am well at presant and hopeing thiss will find you all the same We wer paid too months pay yesterday and I thought I would send a part of it home and enclosed you will find $15 Dolars one dolar over haff of my pay We are haveing very pleasant wether here now warm and quite dry the rail road is repaired and the cars are runing up to Culpepper with suplys now and I would not be suprised if we had a battle soon on the Rapidan soon I think Meed intends to advance and give Lee Battle at some point on the Rapidan before winter sets in witch will be verry soon now I want to have some of you to send me a pair of wolen gloves or mittens gloves if you can get them you can send them by mail for 10 or 15 cts doe them up in a small package and direct the same as a letter When you write again send me a few postage stamps I do not think of annything more to write at presant from your son
                Nelson Taylor

Culpeper C.H. Dec 15th 1863

Dear Sister
      It is only a few days since I wrote

to you but as a good opportunity affords me to write I thought it best to improve it. In my last letter I wrote that we had just got our winter quarters done and exspected to enjoy them for a while but alas a Soldier never has the assureance of where he will be on the morrow even if he is blest with life and health. Well Satterday night there was a Detail of 48 privates and noncomisioned Officers to report the next morning to the Division Q M for duty and I hapened to be one of the lucky ones and we are quartered in a large brick store here in the Vilage of Culpeper and a good stable for our Horses we are near the Depot and the most of our duty is Guarding Quarter Masters and Ordinances Stores Our duty is lighter here than with the regt we have good Quarters and plenty of rations for ourselves and Horses but how long they will permit us to remain here I am not able to say. Perkins and Wadsworth have the shanty alone to themselves 3 men and myself from our Company are here I hear to day they are going to give 10 days furlough 1 out of 50 at a time I am going to try for one but I do not know wether I will succeed in geting one or not. I dont think of annything more at present write as soon as convienant from your Broth
                    N Taylor

PLATE XII

THE PICKET LINE

WINTER 1863-64
KILPATRICK'S RAID

December of 1863 was very cold. The roads had been exceedingly muddy and then frozen solid. One mule had lain down and had been frozen stiff in the mud. About December 17 the War Department issued orders that if 3/4 of a company or regiment would reenlist, they would be sent home in a group with a furlough of 30 days for recruiting. Men having more than 15 months to serve could not reenlist. In addition to the attractive furlough other inducements were offered: U.S. bounty of $402; the N.Y. State bounty of $75; and any local bounties as might be offered.

The men in the field spent the winter in camp near Culpepper with occasional picket duty. On February 6 orders were issued during the night to be ready to move at 7 o'clock in the morning. The best mounted men and a large force of infantry moved toward the Rapidan River. On the 27th a special detail of picked men and horses from several companies was sent to Kilpatrick's command for a raid to Richmond having the objective of liberating Union prisoners.

By the 29th his cavalry units were approaching Richmond which was gearing up to resist. The Federal cavalry were within a few miles of the Confederate capital by March 1, but Kilpatrick failed to assault the outer fortifications which appeared to be very well manned. The cavalry raid failed because of lack of surprise, force, and determination to see it through to successful conclusion. It is now known that Richmond had been defended by inadequate forces and by vigorous attack, might have been taken by Union cavalry.

Culpeper C.H. Dec 16 1863

Dear Father

I have just learnt by the Division Provost Marshal that we can get exspress

matters from washington now by Rail road I though I would have a box of things sent from home and I want a pair of Boots soon and I think the cheepest and best way is to have them sent from home I want a pair of heavey Calf or Kipp skins with heavey sols well nailed good stiff counters legs common length sise 11 and large at that you can get them made and send them as soon as you can with a box of most any thing else you have a mind to send a few pounds of dried fruit 8 or 10 lbs of Butter and some cake dont put any thing in that will spoill and put it in a strong Box and send it as soon as you can I exspect to have a 10 day furlough sometime in February if nothing happens at least I have the promise of one by the Capten The wether is cold here to day and has the apearence of snow you can Direct the Box the same as you do the letters no more at presant from your son
      N Taylor

     Culpeper Va Jan 3rd 1864
Sister Hannah
  I recieved your letter of the 23 in due time and it being Sunday to day I thought it best to write you a few lines to inform you that I am alive and well at presant and hopeing thiss will find you the same. We have not the privialige of

PLATE XIII

A CHRISTMAS DINNER

attending Church as you do in civil life and concequently we spend our time in vairious ways it most always hapens that we have as much if not more duty to do on sunday as anny other day ether on the march or Picketing the hardest fighting we have had we done on Sundays thiss last summer. We have a Chaplain he has been with us 6 months and I dont think he has preached more than 6 sermons to the regt in that time for the reassin we wer on the move or Picketing and if he should preach to day he would not have manny hearers for the wether is verry cold and frosty the coldest we have had thiss Winter Well Christmas and New Years pass off all quiet in camp but we did not have anny luxuries in the way roast Turkeys Chicken pies &C but we had a plenty of Goverment rations when I wrote to you last I was at Culpeper but we came back to the regt Christmas day and a few days ago we thought we would try our skill in cookeing sometimes we draw corn for our horses and we will take some of it to mill and get it ground We mixed up some meal put in some Raisons and sewed it up in a bag and boild it. Well we had a wright smart Puding I recon to use the Sothern frase we have hoe cakes quite often we bake them in a spider we can do most annything in the cooking line if we had the materials to do it with that is all that is lacking. Well 3/4 of our Company has reenlisted enought to hold the Company Organizeation and now there has 9 Companys of the regt have enough to hold the Organizeation of the Regt we have a good many men in the regt that only been in the servis a little over a year and none can reenlist unless they have less than a year to serve nearly all of the old men have reenlisted they are geting ther Pay and a portion of the Bounty to day and they are going home in a few days 6 N.Y. Cavalry started yesterday for home on furlough they are in our Brigade I do not think of annything more at presant enclosed you will find 50^{ct} send me Stamps I havent one to my name and cant get anny here from N. Taylor write soon

    Camp near Culpeper Va Jan 9th1864
Sister Han

    I recieved your letter dated 31 of last month a few days ago just as I was going out on Picket and have not had much time for writing since wer out on Picket 2 days came in to camp night before last and yesterday the Vetrans started for home on 30 days furlough they left here in good sperrits exspecting to have a big time for 30 days and no doubt they will. Our Camp looks as if it was nearly deserted rather lonesom to what it generaly is All that remains of us are in our same quarters we have the horses that the others left to take care of but they are to be turned over to the Division Q Master to day. for the past week we have had very cold wether the coldest I ever saw in this part of the Contry it is quite pleasant to day. I have not got the Box yet all the exspress for the Brigade gets around to Brigade Head quarters about once a week perhaps Il get it some time next week if nothing hapens it cannot get here anny to soon for I want the Boots soon. Well I have not been promoted you wrote as if you thought I had been and I do not exspect to be I had some big promisies if I would reenlist but I could not see the reenlist. Well about the People of culpeper there is but a verry few males very old men and young boys but they are secesh but they are verry glad to take the Oath of Aliegance in Order to get Provision from our Comesariey the inhabitants where ever the armys have traveled are entirely destitute of everry thing you know nothing about war there it is a thing you hear of and read about You wrote that you would like to hapen around sometime when I was cookeing to see me perform well if you should come in to my shanty at this presant time you find me writeing and at the same time macking a ketle of Beef on the fire I intend to

have Roast Beef for Dinner. Well say to Father he must not worry thinking Il enlist for I will not Well I do not think of annything more to write at presant I am well write when conveniant from
                    Nelson Taylor

          Staford Court House Va Jan 11 '64
Dear Father
        As I have nothing to do today I thought I would write a few lines to you again and let you know that I am well at presant and hopeing that thiss will find you all the same the army here not doing much of anything and we exspect to winter here for an army cannot move here in this contry in the winter it is all a horse can do to carry a man the roads are so bad the mud is verry deep and it does not freess hard enought to bare a horse verry often Our horses are nearly starved to death for the want of hay we have been here a month and they have not had but 6 days rations of hay since we have been here 3 days at one time they did not have anything but oak bushes to knaw on but know they get 12 lbs of grain a day and if they do not give us hay soon they will all die for there is not one horse in 5 that will stand the work we do with them over 3 month with all the feed they can eat I thought I would like to have an other

Box of things sent to me the other boys are all geting boxes of good things from home and I think I could use up a box of eatebls to a good advantage now if I had them for it is now trouble to get them now if they are directed wright they want to be Directed the same as the letters and they come to Washing by exspress and then they are sent to Gen Seigles Headquarters and then they are sent to the regt where they are directed to and the exspress must be paid there before it starts I will give you a list of what I want you to send 3 or 4 lb of Butter 6 or 8 lbs of Dried apples some dried Curnts and dried Berrys of any kind some Preserves ½ pound of green Tea and a hand full of sage leaves for tea and if you have any Sausuages send a few pounds and 2 pairs of stockings and as many other good things as you are a mind to tell John and Georges folks if they have any good things that they are afraid will spoill to send it on Be sure and Direct it the same as you do my letters and send it by exspress and pay the Charges on it I will send $10.00 to pay the exspences and I want it sent as soon as you can I do not think of anything more at presant from your son
     Nelson Taylor

Camp near Culpeper Jan 29th 1864
Dear Sister Hannah

I was just thinking it was about time I wrote another letter to the ones at home to inform them that I am among the liveing at presant & enjoying good health my health never was better than it is at the presant time & my apetite is suficeant to consume quite all of my rations My weight is 195 lbs I think it is the heaveyest I ever weight before. Soldiering agrees with my health verry good. You will hardly ever see a Soldier have a cold or a cought unless it is a Recruit one that has just come into the field I think it is because we are exsposed to all kind of weather and we are in the open air all of the time & the changes of the weather does not effect us as it does thoes that live in tight rooms

We are haveing Beautifull weather here at presant it apearrs more like may than it does like January weather there is not anny frost in the ground the the mud is nearly dried up it is allmost uncomfortable warm in the middle of the day especily if we exersis around much I think we will get bad weather enought next month to pay for thiss. We have not had better times since we have been in the servis than what we are haveing thiss winter and especily since the Vetrans went

home we have done no Picketing or Scouting we have nothing but camp duty to do we have mounted drill once a day enought to keep our Horses backs hardened we have a good lot of Horses. I have a Horse that will set himself and me on the other side of a fence or a ditch whenever it is nessesary a Cavalry mans safety depends mostly upon his horse a great many times Well Han I have not got the Box of things witch Father sent me yet If it does not come soon I shall begin to think that I will never get it But I am in hopes it will come with the next lot of exspress for the Brigade. Well I do not think of anny more to write at present give my respects to all and write soon from your Brother
     Nelson Taylor

  Camp near Culpeper Va Feb 4th 1864
Sister Hannah
  I thought it best to write you a few lines again thiss morning to let you know that I am alive & well enjoying myself as well as Soldiers generaly do. We are haveing cold weather with a plenty of wind and mud at presant verry unpleasant but not very cold. We have done no Picket duty for the last month the Cavalry is not doeing but a verry little Picketing thiss winter since the first of Jan and we

are haveing verry comfortable times for Cavalryman I have not got the Box of things that Father sent me and I am about to think that I never will for there is a good many exspress Boxes stolen on the way from washington before they get to where they belong for we have Thieves among Soldiers as well as among Citizens I see that the President has made another call for more troops we want them and must have them the only way to have peace is to have more war first and more war we must have before we can have peace and the more that Party in the north opposes the war and crying for peace instead of bringing peace they are heaping more war upon us. The war has come to that point that the only way it can be settled is by Powder Ball & Sword

    Well Han about my geting a Furlough the prosspect of my geting one is not very encourageing They are not giveing furloughs only to thoes that are reenlisting and over ½ of them have not got theres yet and cannot get them untill thoes come back that are home on furlough now They are verry much disappointed they exspected when they enlisted to get ther furlough immediately but there was so many enlisted it would not do to let them all go at once it would leave to large a gap open here in our army. My bunk mate

has gone to driveing team in the Divisions
Suply train and concequently I am left to
mess alone for the presant I am keeping
Bachelers Hall
Well I do not think of anny thing more to
write at presant I will close hopeing
thiss will find all of you well at home.
write soon my love to all from your
Brother
               Nelson Taylor

  Camp near Culpeper Va Feb 8th 64
Sister Han
    Your letter of the 3 of thiss month
is at hand & was glad to hear that you was
well at home., The exspress Bill was in
the letter I have not got the Box yet I
wrote a letter the first of thiss month to
one of my old mess mates in washington one
that was wounded last August in the
Brandy Station fight to see if my Box was
there or not or wether they had recieved
and fowarded it on too the army and I have
not had an ansswer yet but I will in a day
or two Our quiet slumbers wer awakened 4
oclk on the morning of the 5th by the
drums in the Infantry camp sounding the
Long roll & the Cavalry Bugle Blowing
Boots and Saddles and we had orders to
march at daylight Well daylight found the
Army of the Potomac moveing towards the
Rapidan Our Division went off on the

right Flank and we came up to the River at Barnetts Ford the first day and halted for the night our regt what there is of us was sent out on Picket for the night we wer called in in the morning the first Brigade attempted to cross the river at the ford but wer repulsed by Infantry & Artillry on the other side the fighting was done mostly by Artillry we had 4 pieces the Rebs had 6 that they used. The first Brigade lost 20 kild and wounded 4 kild they done what fighting there was we layed there till noon and then we started back and we arived here in our old quarters about 8 P.M. The Infantry went out to the Rapidan Station they had some canonadeing but I have not heard what they did do I see they are back in there camps again thiss morning. We wer out too days 1 night it rained a verry little the first day and verry muddy did not get much sleep the ground is to cold and wet to sleep warm I got a couple hours sleep on Soldiers Feathers that is 2 rails I do not think it best to write anny more thiss time from your Brother
    Nelson Taylor

  Camp near Culpeper Va Feb 16th
Sister Han
  I find myself writeing a few lines to you at home thiss morning to inform you

that I am well at presant and wishing
thiss will find you the same. I have been
in the Saddle most of the time for 3 days
past. yesterday our Division was Reviewed
and Inspected by the Division Comander Gen
Merrett near Culpeper It was a warm
pleasant day and there was a large crowed
of Spectators from the Infantry camps wer
on hand to see the show. Sunday morning
our regt and 1 squadron of the 17 Va
Cavalry wer ordered to go and burn a
Disstillery about 2 miles out side of the
pickets on the Sperryville Pike we went
out and Burnt it and captured 2 prisoners
one was a Captain of a noted Party of
Bushwhackers in that vicinity the same
gang has shott a number of our Pickets
thiss winter on the Pike We came back to
camp and had Orders to be ready at 8 oclk
in the morning for Grand Review of the
Cavalry Corps on the plains of
Steavensburgh By the Corps Commander.
Well we went over there and had the Review
and a snowstorm to come back to camp in
we are haveing cold stormy weather now
Well I have not got the Box yet and do not
think I will get it now It is not in the
exspress office at washington it was sent
out to the army and it has been lost here
in the army. there is a good many of
them stolen by the guards I will send the
exspress bill back in thiss letter for it

is of no use to me here and I do not think it is worth anny thing to you for the Exspress company is not holding for anny loss after they deliver them over to the Govertment at washington. Well I do not think of anny thing more to write at presant from your Brother
N. Taylor

Camp near Culpeper Va Mar 4 1864
Dear Sister

As I have not had a letter from Home in sometime I thought it best to write and see why some of you are not writing a letter to your Soldier Boy away off down in Dixie Well I am well & enjoyeing myself as well as Soldiering will permit off. You will see perhaps before thiss reaches you of the Cavalry movements witch is being enactted at thiss presant time from the Army of the Potomac I was thinking you would be anxious to hear from me & I find myself writeing a few lines thiss morrning Our Cavalry is nearly all of it are out makeing a Raid on the Flank and Rear of Gen. Lee army and we have heard nothing reliable from them since they left 5 days ago and we are quite anxious to hear with what success they have met with some of our regt is out with them. I went over to Brandy Station Satterday and when I returned they had

gone out and that is the reason that I am not out with them. Our Vetran Volenteers have returned havein had a good time on furlough & now comes the tug of war for 3 years   I see no way of geting a 10 day Furlough since the reenlisting come up and I will have to wait and take one as long as I want it Well I do not get the Box yet and I gess that it is among the missing. I think I writen enought for thiss time write soon from your Brother
                    Nelson Taylor

     Camp near Culpeper Va Mar 9th 1864
Sister Hannah
     Your letter of March the 1st was recieved in due time & read with much interest as all Soldiers do there Letters from Home Well han your letter found me well and enjoyeing good health as usuual and a plenty of the nessefary of life on hand to make us comfortable. You wanted to know what I done for Boots whether I had a good pair or not yes I have a good pair I bought them some 2 weeks ago for witch I Paid 9.00 Dolars Borrowed money at that We have 4 months Pay due us now we will get it the 15th of thiss month. Our paymaster was here last month and payed all the rest of the Brigade except our regt. Our Clothing account of 1863 was not made out as it should be some way.

we have to square up with the Govertment for our Clothing at the end of the year I have not drawn as much as they allow me quite Capt. Corrigan of our Company has been Promoted to Major Lieut. H. W, Mason of Company G promoted to Capt. of our Company is well pleased with the change. Mother wanted to know who our Col. Gen was Col. W^{m}Sackett Lieut Col. G. Nichols are our Colonel we have 3 majors Corrigan, Bently and Denning. Brigadier Gen. Merrett comands the Division now Col. Deavons of the 6 N Y Cavalry commands the Brigade he has had command of the Brigade nearly a year now. I presume you at home have an idea that a Soldiers life is all hardships sufferings of all kinds Glomy low speriteted and every thing else to make one miserryable Well I can say that I have never saw anny of that kind of Soldiering yet it is verry true we get rather hungry some times and pretty cold at other tims but that dont last long we soon get around where we are suplyed. I am perfectly contented where I am and I think I am just where I should be untill thiss Rebelion is put down and Slavery emancipated and I am confident it will be accomplished in due time it may be 1 2 or 3 years yet of war to accomplish it. Well I think I have writen enought for this time write soon from your Broth

Camp near Culpeper Va March 15th 1864

Dear Father

It being sometime since I have writeing to you I thought it best to do so thiss morning as I had some money to send to you. We wer Paid 4 months pay Yesterday we are paid up to the 1st of march now We settled up our Clothing account for 1863 I had $11.50 worth of Clothing due me I was paid the amount due me yesterday

You will find twenty Dolars in thiss letter if it goes through all right and nothing happens to it and you can give me Credit for the same Write as soon as you can after recieveing thiss and let me know if it went through safe. Well I have no news to write about the Army is all quiet in there quarters except the Cavalry that is off with Gen Killpatrick and they are exspected here to day they are on there way from Alixandria to thiss place they came on Transports from Fortress Monroe to Alixandria I do not get the Box yet and probly I never will write soon from your son

                    Nelson Taylor

    Camp near Culpeper Va Mar 24th 1864

Dear Sister Han

    Your letter of the 20 is at hand and

read with much interest I was glad to hear
that you wer all well at Home & glad to
hear that the money I sent had safely
reached its destination We had a severe
snow storm here on the afternoon and
evening of the 22nd, the snow was verry
near 1 ft. deep yesterday morning and
verry cold it was the nearest to winter
weather that we have had before thiss
winter   It came off warm to day and the
snow has nearly all disapeared allready.
I see that George has improved greately in
writeing or else he had some one to help
him I gess if I mistake not he had Ma to
help him how I would like to see him and
all of you but if I live it will only be a
short time before I will report there for
duty   How quick time pases away It does
not seam posible that I have been a
Soldier too years and one half but so it
is Time waits for no one war or no war.
Well you said they wer trying to get an
instrument in the church at Clifton Park.
Wel I dont know but it is all right enough
to have some Instrumental music with the
Vocal but I never did fancy music in
church I would say to the young men there
if they are fond of instrumental music to
join Uncle Samuels Choire and they will be
suplyed immediately with instruments full
of noise and they do not require much
exertion to get music out of them only by

faceing the Music. Han you said you was glad you had no Boys large enough to go to the war well now it is not so with me if I had a ½ dosen Boys I should want them right here in the ranks for if your Contry is not worth fighting for it is not worth haveing well enough of thiss for the presant I was somewhat suprised to heare such a report from John Peck Higgins well there is a great many of the young men on the same road to ruin. But I thank God that I am free from the Intockcicating drink Swearing & Gambleing and my prayer is that he will shield me from them. Han you wanted me to have my Picture taken and sent to you I exspect to have some Photographs to morrow and if I get them I will send 1 or more in thiss letter I have just wrote on to John and will not send it off till I get the Photographs I want to send him one Well it is verry near midnight and I guess that I have writen nearly enought for thiss time one of my Bunk Mates is asleep R.B. Wadsworth White he is on horse guard. there is only 3 of us in the shanty now I have a good warm fire in our fire place I wish you could just step in and take a view of the shanty and its inhabitants part of our company are out on Picket well I wont write anny more untill I get the Photographs good night

March 28th If you get thiss letter you will find enclosed 2 Photographs you can keep one for yourself and the other for Mother I have sent George & John one write as soon as you have time no more at presant my love to all from your Broth
      Nelson Taylor
Send me a few more Stamps when you write again

GRANT AND SHERIDAN

At the end of February Congress revived the rank of Lieutenant General, a grade formerly accorded only to George Washington. On March 1, President Lincoln nominated General Ulysses S. Grant for the post. General Grant declared the objective of the Army of the Potomac was to confront and defeat Lee and his army issuing campaign orders that the Army of the Potomac was to find and defeat Lee's army: "Wherever Lee goes, there you will go also." To that end the balance of the month of March and practically all of April were devoted to painstaking preparations for the campaign.

Major General Sheridan was selected to command the Cavalry Corps, a duty he assumed after General Pleasanton was relieved and General Buford had died of typhoid fever. Sheridan reviewed his new command and while he found the health and equipment of the men very good, the horses were thin and worn down by the picket duty of a continuous line of nearly sixty miles. He knew that the command's effectiveness depended on the strength of its horses and the extensive picketing was unnecessary and wasteful of resources. The cavalry should focus on fighting the enemy's cavalry, and to that end he reorganized the command.

Camp near Culpeper Va April 17th 64

Sister Hannah

I have recieved your letter of April 10 a day or two since I had just came in from 5 days Picketing and have been quite busy since and not being in a writeing mood untill now. Well your letter found me well as usual We have had a great deal of rain here for the last few weeks and it has done some damage with our Rail Road

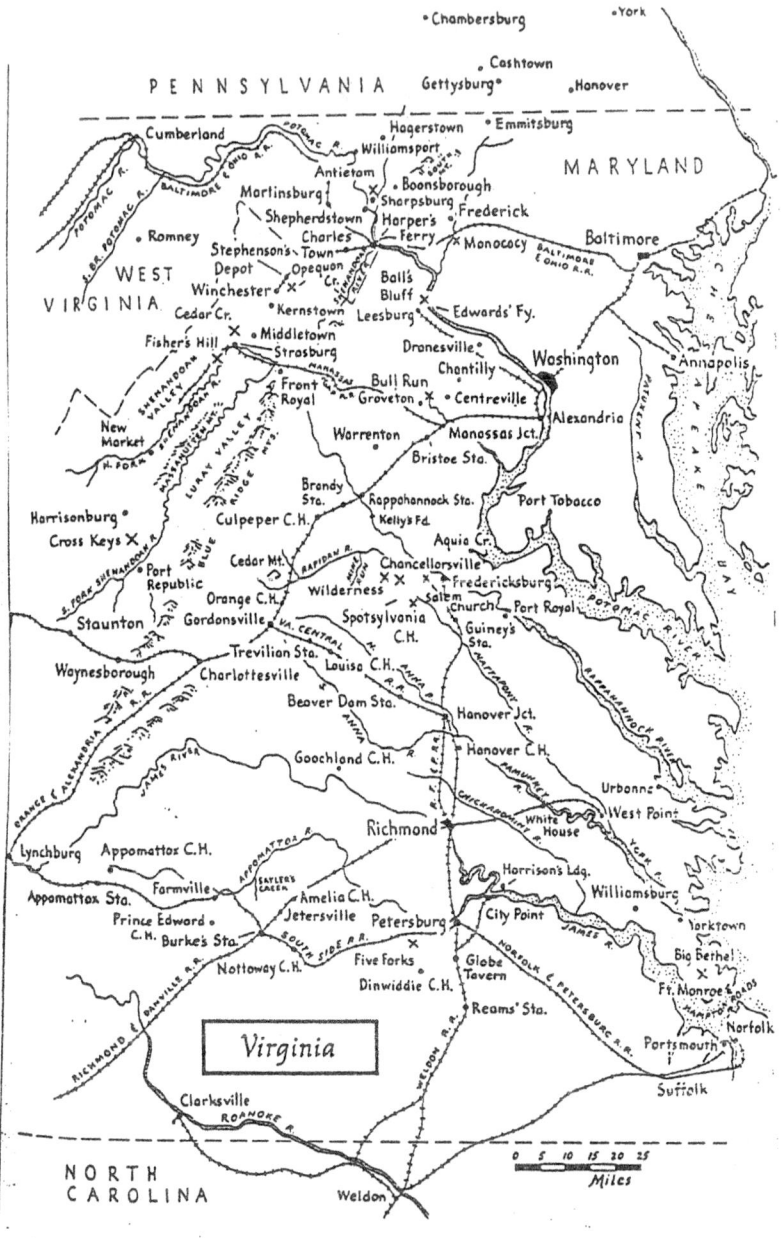

Bridges 2 of them wer swept away they are rebuilt now so the trains are runing again in your letter I found an Express bill saying that my Box had been Delivered at Culpeper in Jan to a Sergt of the 2nd U S. Cavalry who recieves all express for our Division I went there sometime in Febuary to see about it He recieves all Exspress for the Division from the Express Co He gives receipts for so manny Boxes and Packages 1 or 2 car loads at a time and as it is unloaded that witch belongs to each Brigad is piled up by itself and hauled off to Brigade Head Quarters and there it is sorted over for the regt I think my Box has been sent off to some other Brigade and thoes that had the handling of it see it did not belong there and they have keeped it for ther own use I cannot hold anny one responsible for it after it leaves the Express companys hands I will go over and see about it again as soon as I can get a pass the Army is about moveing we are exspecting the word march now everry day and no Passes are given unless the most urgent reassons are given by thoes that want one. I think the Box and Contents are used up long before thiss and perhaps it has done some boddy some good. But it would be some satisfaction to know who has got it. Well I have not much to write thiss time and concequently thiss will have to sufice for thiss time I was thinking it would be a good Idea for me to send you the names of some of our Company in case annything should happen to me you could write to them I will comence first with the Capt H. W. Masson Lieut J. Burrows or R. B. Martin Harmmon. M. O. Brasted it will be well enought to remember these names for future use provideing it would be nesesary to do so no more at presant N. Taylor

                Culpeper Va April 25 1864
Sister Hannah
    I thought it best for me to write a few lines to you at home again as I have time to do so thiss afternoon The Army of the Potomac has not made a move yet and we are in our old quarters at presant and the troops are all busy Drilling Target Shooting and having Reveiws & Inspecttions and it keeps us busy the most of the time There has been some changes made in our Cavalry dureing the Reorganiseation of the Army Major Gen. Sheridan Comands the Corps Gen Pleasanton has gone to the Western Army Brigade.....

(The corner portion of this letter is missing. The transcription continues where lines are complete.)

.....nearly one half of the men in our Division is Dismounted and cannot get Horses to mount them and they will have to serve on foot some thiss summer I have a good Horse and I think he will last me a few months yet We are haveing pleasant weather here now the wind is nearly dryed up and if the weather holds so a few days longer we will be on the move. We have 15 days Rations on our Waggons of Hard Tack Sugar, Coffee, and Salt. we will get no meat only Beef tho and will be Driven along and kild ....

     Mitchel Station Va May 2nd 64
Sister Han
  You will see by the heading of thiss letter that we have changed our location. We moved out of our old camp last Tuesday and came to thiss place on the Rail Road between Culpeper and the Rapidan since our Division is encamped here at presant the first and second Brigades have been here all winter. We have been verry bussy the past week. Our Brigade went out to Madison Court House last Wednesday and found only one Company of the 10 Va Cavalry there Picketing. We captured 5 of them and the rest got out of the way. We returned to camp the same night some what Fatigued not being in the Saddle much of late. We are haveing warm and pleasant

weather here now Fruit trees are all in Bloom and everrything tells us that Summer is close upon us   May 3rd I comenced thiss yesterday and got so far and then I was Detaild to go to Brandy Station after Horses for our Regt our regt is nearly all Mounted now and readdy for action and I have no doubt but what we will have enought to do soon Well Han I have not much to write about thiss time I am well at presant and enjoyeing myself well enought no more at presaant write soon my love to all

Nelson Taylor

THE WILDERNESS, SPOTTSYLVANIA, JAMES RIVER

With the appointment of Ulysses S. Grant as Lieutenant General with total responsibility for all the land forces of the North, the Civil War entered upon the final act of the long, bloody conflict.

Early on May 4, the Army of the Potomac moved against Lee who was entrenched on the south bank of the Rapidan River. This was destined to be the big push by the Federal Army and to culminate at Appomattox.

Grant decided to cross the Rapidan at Germana and Ely's Fords and head directly for Richmond. The Army of the Potomac was at peak strength: three big infantry units; Sheridan's strong cavalry of about 10,000; 318 pieces of artillery; and 65 miles of wagon train of more than 400 wagons. Grant had in excess of 120,000 well-fed, clothed, and equipped men with high morale. In contrast Lee had only about 62,000 men and 224 artillery pieces. However, Lee was confident, for he knew that Grant's massive columns would have to travel through the Wilderness, a tangled jungle, terrain so difficult to traverse that superiority in numbers would not count.

Reveille alerted the cavalry at 5 a.m. on May 5 with orders to be ready to march. The 9th went on picket on the road toward Banks Ford. Grant decided to put his columns in motion to clear the Wilderness area and get his army to the high open ground near Spottsylvania C.H. Sheridan's corps fought the enemy for possession of the crossroads at Todd's Tavern. Here the 9th cavalry dismounted and fighting on foot, drove the enemy back three miles into a thicket of pines and then sheltered themselves behind trees along the edge of the woods. On Sunday, May 8, the dismounted cavalry again opposed Jeb Stuart's cavalry near Todd's Tavern in ferocious combat. The 9th lost six men killed, seventeen wounded, and four captured.

(The following entry appears in the official records of the 9th NYSV Cavalry: Taylor, Nelson, age 22 .... wounded in action at Todd's Tavern, Va., May 8, '64.)

Early on May 9 Sheridan's Cavalry Corps marched on the plank road toward Fredericksburg from a position between Spottsylvania Court House and Chancellorsville. They crossed the Mattapony and North Anna Rivers. One division moved on to Beaver Dam Station to cut the Virginia Central Railroad. Before reaching the Station, the division recaptured about four hundred Union prisoners who had been taken in the Wilderness.

On the 11th one brigade marched to Ashland Station to cut the Fredericksburgh and Richmond Railroad. The 5th Virginia Cavalry opposed the advance but were beaten back. General Stuart was mortally wounded in this battle. Taking advantage of General Sheridan's control of the road to Richmond, the 9th was directed to move to Meadow Bridge and cross the Chickahominy. This they did on the 14th and reached Malvern Hill. Here the corps found ample forage and rations. On May 17 orders were received to march; horses were saddled but soon unsaddled as the command did not start. At dark the bugles blew "boots and saddles" again and the command marched all night and nearly all the next day. Sheridan decided to cross the Pamunkey at White House on pontoons. The 9th NY, while Sheridan was waiting for the pontoons, marched to New Castle and Hanovertown to picket the fords. On the 22nd the whole command crossed, moving to Milford Station on May 24 and 25 where they obtained feed, rations, fresh clothing, and three weeks' accumulated mail.

Sheridan's independent cavalry movements were highly successful: Meade had been able to move his enormous trains with relative freedom; the harassment of Lee's rear by the cavalry had compelled him to retreat toward Richmond; the Confederate Cavalry had been defeated at Yellow Tavern.

PLATE XIV

THROUGH THE WILDERNESS

Malvern Hill Va May 15th 64

Dear Father

It is some time since I have writen home and I supose you are lookeing for some news from me I am alive and well at presant We left our camp at Mitchel Station on the 4 of thiss month and we have been marching & Fighting every day since and nights not excepted and yesterday we halted here on Malvern Hill near James River where we are getting Rations & Forage witch we needed verry much before we got here. We had some hard fighting on 6, 7 & 8 of thiss month on the left Wing of Meads Army we wer near Tods Tavern Our regt lost upwards of 50 kild wounded & mising our lost 1 kild 2 wounded 3 missing On the night of the 8 our Cavalry Corps concentrated on the Fredricksburgh & Chancellersvill Plank Road 8 Miles from Fredricksburgh and the next morning we started on a Raide in the rear of lees Army we Cut the Gordonsvill & Richmond R. Road at Beaver Dam Station and Burnt a large quanty of Comesary stores 2 Engines and a lot of carrs and tore up 1 mile of track On the 11 we cut the Fredricksburgh & Richmond and Destroyed a little over a mile of the track and there we had a sharpe fight in the afternoon and our force being the strongest we soon cleard the road on the

Malvern Hill Va May 15th 64

Dear Father

It is some time since I have writen home and I supose you are lookeing for some news from me I am alive and well at presant We left our camp at Mitchel Statiers on the 4 of this month and we have been marching & Fighting every day since and nights not excepted and yesterday we halted here on Malvern Hill near James River where we are getting Rations & Forage witch we needed verry much before we got here. We had some hard fighting on 6, 7 & 8 of this month on the left Wing of Meads Army we is cornear Tods Tavern Our regt lost upwards of 50 Kild wounded & missing our

12 we had a sharp fight crossing the Chicohomny swamp Major Corrigan Was wounded in left leg badly had to be Amputated We came down through Mecanicksvill, Gains Mills Bottoms Bridge to Malvern hill wer McClelans old Battle grounds We have not heard from Meeads Army yet do not know how they are makeing it When we left Meead was whiping lee at all points I do not exspect to stop here long. It is rumored we are to cross the James river to night and make a Raid out towards North Carolina Well I have not time to write anny more now I am well at Presant give my love to all from your Son
       Nelson Taylor

 Write soon Direct the same as you have it will come to us some time we have had no mail since the 3rd

    Camp 9. N.Y. Cavalry May 25, 64 in the Woods 8 miles from Hanover Junction
Dear Sister Han.

I have just recieved your letter of May 16th the first mail we have had thiss month and I thought it best to write an answer and trust to luck for haveing a chance to send it off I wrote a letter to Father the 15 of thiss month we wer then on Melvarn Hill near the James River on Gen Sheridans Raid I think you have seen the particulars of the Raid in the papers before thiss Well, I can say that we have done a goodeal of Marching and Fighting thiss month and we are ready to do more. We had hard fighting on the 6, 7, 8 of this month not far from Spottsylvania C. House we lost quite a number there. Company I lost 4 prisoners, 1 badly wounded died afterwards one of thoes that wer taken prisoner we knew was wounded and the others we knew nothing of at that time and when our army took Spottsylvania Court House they found a lot of our Wounded there in a Hospital one of our Company was among them his name T. G. Histed and we learnt from him that one of the other boys was mortally wounded and died the other 2 are suposed to be prisoners It was on the 7 we had the hardest fighting and when we lost thees men we wer Dismounted and fighting in a thick piece of wood, and we found them to much for us and it was nearly dark and we had to fall back ½ mile our Regt lost about 40 men that day and the next morning at daylight we advanced again and found they had a strong position and Infantry suport and we halted and wer soon relieved by our Infantry Our Cavalry Corp Concentrated that day about 12 miles from Fredricksburgh and camped for the night and Drew 3 days Rations and wer told they would have to last us 6 days and perhaps longer Well the next morning we marched and at dark we found ourselves at Beaver Dam Station in the Rear of Lees Army. Burning his suplys 2 Engines over 100 cars, tore up nearly 1 mile track Burnt the ties laid the rails on top and as soon as they got hot they would bend so they could not be used We Recaptured 300 of our prisoners and a number of rebs We marched the next morning towards Richmond and camped that night on the South Anna River we marched again the next morning and struck the Richmond & Fredricksburgh R. R. at Hungary Station 10 miles from Richmond we found nothing there only the tracks and we Destroyed 1½ miles of that in less than one hour. We had met with no force of the Enemy to hinder our march up to thiss time We went ahead again only about 2 miles to Alans Cross Roads and there the Head of our Column ran onto the Head of Stuarts Column of reb Cavalry they wer on our left and both wer trying to get to the Crossroads first and hold it. Well 1 Brigade of the rebs got there first but they did not stop there long our Brigade was Dismounted and we charged on them they wer Dismounted and in to deep Ditch in the Road. Our regt hapened to get in front of the same Regt 5 Va Cavalry that cut our Regt up at Spottsylvania only a few days before we formed our line in the woods and advanced and we had a field to crosed before we came to the Road where they wer perhaps a hundred Rods in width we started on Double quick under a heavy fire of Carbines and 2 pieces of Artillry. Well we crossed the Field and over the fence and about the time we wer geting into the road they wer geting out as fast as they knew how our Regt took 92 priseners and the most of them belong to the 5th Va Cav. Kild the Col.1 Capt and took 4 other officers of the same regt priseners Our regt only lost 2 kild some 3 or 4 Wounded. We halted in the road and the first Brigade in our Division Brigadier Gen Custer came up Mounted and charged them with the Saber and took 2 pieces of Artillery and 30 od priseners and drove them back a mile or two on the same road they came on. we had one man of our company wounded that day We stoped there till nearly 2 oclk in the morning before we started and at daylight we found ourselves 2½ miles from Richmond and took a turn to the left on the Road to Medow Bridge when our advance reached the bridge it was torned up and Guarded by rebs from the other side 2 Brigades of our Division was Dismounted and sent acrossed the Bridge and we found the same Brigade we fought with the day before we had quite a shorp fight with them before they would leave there position Our Pionners soon fixted the Bridge so it was safe to crosse. About the same time we crossed the bridge and comenced fighting the Rebs made an Attack on our rear with 3 regts of Infantry and a lot of Home Guards and a part of Stuarts Cavalry and I can tell you things looked rather scarely about that time in an enemys contry and fighting in rear & front at the same time But we had a good position to check a strong force in the rear and Gen. Sheridan proved himself to be a good Gen. We had 24 pieces of Artillery with us and he placed 22 of them where the rebs could not see them untill they got close upon them the other 2 pieces wer with the rear guard and keeped falling back and the rebs massed ther force and charged but did not come far before our Artillery opened on them with Grape and there Ranks wer thined out and the ground was rather thick with ther dead they Rallied and made the attemped again but with no better sucess. Gen Stuart was wounded in that fight and died in a day or two after the rebs lost 350 kild & wounded there that day Major Corrigan of our regt was wounded in the leg and had to have it Amputated the rebs did not trouble us anny more to speak of that day thiss was the 12th day we marched to

Gains Mills and camped for the night on McClellans old Battle grounds and we marched the next day to Bottoms Bridge. next day to Melvarn Hill near James river. Our Gun Boats saw us and threw 3 shells at us before our Signal Corp told them who we wer we wer out of Hard tack and did not get anny untill the next day but we do not go hungry wen we are in the enemys contry if we can find annything to eat we had a plenty of fresh meat Bacon and corn meal we cooked our own Hoe Cake We drew 5 days Rations & 3 days forage I wrote a letter to father when there the 15th we marched from there to the White House landing stated the 17, and got there on the night of the 18th and camped 2 nights one day the 20 our Division was sent up the Pahmunky river and the first Brigade went far enought to burn a Railroad Bridge near Hannover Court Hous. we got back to the White House 21 at noon we Drew 5 days rations and crossed the river at night and marched up through King William Co and came into the lines of the Army of the Potomac to day about noon and the first Infantryman we saw wer thoes that we Recaptured at Beaver Dam Station they went down the James river and up to washington and wer on there way to the front to join there regt they give us some Hearty Cheers today as well as they did when we released

them Well I must bring thiss letter to a Halt for it is nearly midnight my candle most burnt and I think a nap will do me good our troops droved the rebs across the North Anna last night fighting all day to day rebs falling back. We have had News Papers only once thiss month 13 & 14 dates dont know what is going on only what little one can see cant see much here I got a letter from Alidia and Fanny Taylor to day tell them will write as soon as I can write often give my love to all write soon.
Gen Grant is going to fight it out thiss Summer there never was known such fighting as has been done here thiss I think we will clean them out of Va thiss summer from Nelson Taylor

9 N.Y. Cavalry Army Potomac Va. June 5th
Dear Sister Hannah

As I have a chance or sending out mail to day I thought it best to write a few lines again to you at home to inform you that I am well at presant and hope thiss will find you the same I wrote you a letter the 25th of May I think you must of recieved it before thiss we had then just returned from the Raid and wer near Hanover Junction and we have been in the Saddle nearly every day since we have done a goodeal of marching and some fighting

and as to that we had a plenty of both.
Our Cavalry had some hard fighting the 27,
28 near Hannover Ferry on the Pamunky
river after we laid Pontoons Bridge and
crossed over thiss side Our regt was not
engaged ether day only one Squadron had a
skirmish 1 man kild one woundded the 2nd
Division was on our left and done the most
of the fighting We had to hold the
crosing untill our Infantry came down Our
Division had a fight on the 30, near New
Castle we had just camped and unsaddled
wer washing and grazeing our Horses they
wer loose and we wer takeing things cool
but the Rebs could not let us rest they
drove in our Pickets Well we saddled and
wer ready for them in time but none to
soon We had a hard fight for a few hours
but we gave them all they wanted and drove
them back they wer a Division of Cavalry
just from South Carolina they fight better
than Stuarts Cavalry can or at least
better then they have done thiss spring.
Our Company had 2 men wounded 1 kild in
the regt and several wounded. Our
Division had a fight the first day of this
month near Coal Harbor our Regt was not
engaged but was under fire part of the
time suporting a Battery. Our Cavalry
had Orders to hold the position untill the
Infantry could get there they came up and
relieved us after 4 hours with hard

fighting to do it with Reb Infantry to contend June 2nd we marched down to Bottoms Bridge on the Chicahominy and the Rebs wer oposed to our crosing there they opened there Artillery on us but without any damage being done we went into camp out of shelling distance and laid there 2 nights and 1 day and yesterday morning our Division marched back to New Castle and camped there last night thiss morning we saddled and march about 8 miles we are now on the right flank of our Army and about 6 miles from Medow Bridge and a plenty of rebs in our front between us and the Chickahomny. I saw the 77th N. Y. Regt a few days ago and I saw Elihu Jones Peter Simmons there regt has lost heavily in the late Battles. We do not get anny News Papers and do not know but a very little of what is being done even here in the Army only what little one can see and hear and that is not much. Well I think of nothing more at present only write soon and oftener we get mail once in 3 or 4 days now my love to all from your Broth Nelson Taylor

TREVILLIAN STATION RAID

On June 5, 1864, General Meade ordered General Sheridan to take two divisions of cavalry to destroy the railroad bridge over the Rivanna River and the railroad from there through Gordonsville toward Hanover Junction. On June 6 the two divisions were at New Castle Ferry. The supply of both horses and men was depleted due to the severe service over the past month. Three days' rations were issued to the men and two days' feed for the horses. Each trooper was to carry his own rations and forty rounds of ammunition with the grain on the pommel of the saddle. The divisions also carried enough canvas covered boats to make a small pontoon bridge.

On the 10th the enemy and Gregg's division met on the Louisa Court House road where the enemy was posted behind barricades in dense timber about three miles from Trevillian. Cheney reports that Sheridan rode up to Devin, a brigade commander, and asked if he had a regiment that could break the enemy's line in the woods. Devin replied "Yes -- -- I have. Where's the 9th N.Y.?" Promptly the 9th rode to the front, dismounted, and formed line facing the woods, with Col. Sackett in command. The effective force of the regiment was about two hundred and twenty officers and men. When Sackett gave the "Forward" command, the men sprang into the woods with a yell. Col. Sackett and about forty men fell before the fire of the enemy, but the balance of the regiment forced on to the enemy's lines and drove them back out of the woods. The regiment pressed on taking over 80 prisoners, many of whom testified to the heroic daring of the 9th in breaking their line.

When the regiment arrived at the station, a Confederate wagon loaded with ammunition with its four mules in harness was standing awaiting its teamster. A Confederate flag was found in this wagon. (Could this be the flag Nelson refers to in his letter of June 25?) Some 380 prisoners were taken there. The Union forces proceeded to tear up the railroad track for some distance toward Gordonsville. Because of the dwindling supply of ammunition, another engagement was too great a risk, and Sheridan withdrew on the night of June 12. The losses in the 9th N.Y. were the largest of any engagement during the war: about 300 killed and captured in addition to the wounded. Due to the scarcity of ambulance wagons, the wounded had to be transported in old buggies, carts, and any other available vehicle. The suffering of the wounded was intense, the heat of the summer and dusty roads adding to their discomfort.

June 20 the corps moved to the Pamunkey opposite White House to obtain feed, rations, and ammunition. Two days later, Torbert's Division was sent to secure Jones Bridge on the Chickahominy. On June 24 the division moved toward Charles City Court House where Gregg was established to protect the wagon trains. Here the men stood to horse all night. On the 26th and 27th the wagons were ferried across the James River.

On the afternoon of June 29 the 9th responded to "Boots and saddles" and marched to Prince George Court House where the men stood to horse all night. On July 1 the corps marched two or three miles toward the Weldon railroad; back to Prince George Court House on the 2nd; back to James River on the 3rd where the weary men and horses went into camp near Light House Point. Boat loads of supplies, including pickles, canned and fresh fruits, were brought there by the Christian and Sanitary Commissions and distributed.

The 4th of July was observed at City Point by a display of national colors, a national salute by one gunboat, and fireworks at City Point.

Cheney reports that in the sixty days since leaving Culpeper, the regiment had been across the country from the Rappahannock to the James River three times, had been up near Gordonsville and back, and recently way below

Petersburg, and back to the James. The men had bathed in nearly every river, brook, and rivulet between the Rapidan and the Blackwater, had crossed and helped to destroy much of every railroad, and in the aggregate had met and fought the enemy nearly half of those days, besides picketing and patrolling many roads and guarding many fords. Since no pack mules and very few wagons had been allowed to the cavalry for transportation since June 6, all the men had been reduced to the scantiest necessities for clothing and articles for comfort and cleanliness. The cavalry remained in the vicinity of Light House Point near City Point until the 26th resting and recuperating. Here they drew new clothing, and about 1,500 horses were received.

At this point in the conduct of the Civil War, Congress passed legislation forbidding payment to men in the cavalry service who owned their horses and for which they had been drawing 40¢ per day. The quartermaster was authorized to purchase all private horses. The records show that the highest price paid was $185 with prices ranging down to $100.

On July 28 the cavalry was scouting on the New Market and Central roads. A Confederate division advanced to attack the Union line and bullets began to fall among Torbert's men standing to horse. The command was given to form dismounted. As the 9th moved forward, General Torbert asked "What regiment is that?" Col. Devin replied "The 9th NY. You will hear them yell directly. They are going to charge." "Did you order a charge?" "No," answered Devin, "but they were never in line five minutes without charging." They did, and opened with rapid carbine fire when within short range. The enemy halted and then faced about and retreated rapidly with the men of the 9th using their carbines and revolvers with deadly effect. The 9th lost only one killed and three wounded while the enemy suffered sixty dead, sixty-three prisoners and two battle flags captured from the 28th North Carolina.

Before daylight on July 30 Torbert's division moved to the south side of the River, recrossing the Appomattox. The cavalry was on the move night and day of July 30 and 31, and on Sunday, August 1, returned to camp near City Point greatly fatigued by the strenuous service, lack of sleep, and the excessive heat.

By now the Confederates were constantly making raids and menacing Washington because of their possession of the Shenandoah Valley. General Sheridan was given command of a newly reorganized force and given instructions for the military movement and for conducting the campaign in the Shenandoah Valley.

On Picket near White House Landing
Alans Point June 22nd June 25, 1864
Dear Sister

I have not writen letters to you at home since the first of thiss month for the reasson is we have had no opportunity of sending out any mail and I am not sure of haveing a chance of sending thiss of verry soon but I thought I would write you a few lines and when an opportunity of sending mail I would have it readey. I am glad that I can say that I am alive and well at present and hope thiss will find you the same. We started from the Army of the Potomac on an expedition the 7 of this month Gen Sheridan with the 1st & 2nd Divisions crossed the Pahmunkey at New Castle ferry and we went up through King William & Spotsylvania County and struck Richmond & Gordonsville R. Road 9 miles from the latter place at Trevillion

Station on the 11th and there we found Gen. Hampton Cavalry Stuarts old comand and we had a verry hard fight and we drove them from ther position on the R. R. and held it our Regt was engaged about 2 hours and lost 51 men Kild Wounded and missiing Col. Sacket was Mortally Wounded not much hope of his recoverry and one man Wounded and died in a few hours our Company suffered the least of any in the regt it was one of the hardest Cavalry fights of the war we had posession of the Battle field and on the morning of the 12th a portion of our forces went to destroying the R. Road and they made a clean work for 4 miles and late in the afternoon we atacked them again and found them in Rifle Pits where we could not drive them out verry well and at dark we comenced falling back We had to leave some of our Wounded behind all of the worst cases we left. The Rebs claim that they whiped us there but I dont see it so it is now about an even thing We captured and brought away over 400 prisoners and we lost about the same amount I captured a Battle flag it was in a wagon that broke down in ther flight it was loaded with Amunition it belong to the 5. S. Carolina Cavelry. Well we turned our line of march backward to join the Army of the Potomac On June 18th we arived at King & Queen Court

House about 15 miles above West Point and our Wounded and Prisoners we sent to West Point from there for transportation Our Wounded had a hard time being 7 days on the road and it is verry hot and dry I never saw it so dry before it is enought to kill a well man 19th we went back up the Matepony river to Dunkirk and laid our Pontoons and camped there for the night the next day we crossed and marched to the White House Landing and found that the Army had changed there baise over onto James river all but our Corp Trains wer there and 3 regt of Infantry and a Gunboat to guard it the same day we arrived ther Hampton Cavalry made there apearance and thought they would capture it but the Gunboat soon made them fall back to a safe distance On the morning of the 21 we crossed the river and found Hamptons Cavalry near by and in the afternoon we atacked them to find out there positions I supose and had quite a fight for an hour and Major Bently of our 1Regt was Wounded in leg and had it amputated and 3 men of Co A Wounded We wer on Picket that night and the next morning they had left our front dureing the night. Our Brigade marched that day to Jones Bridge on the Chickahomny and camped for the night the rest of our Cavalry went of on our right and had some fighting dureing the day we wer with our Train and we layed there untill the next day about noon when our regt was sent to open communication with the Gunboats on the James river by way of Charles City C. House the Distance from Jones Bridge to James river 10 miles C. House 4 miles and we Picketed there untill the next day when our train came up Our Cavalry had fighting all of the way from the White House through to the James river where we are now at Alans Point. I comenced writeing thiss letter the 22nd and have been writeing a few lines at a time so to have a letter to send out when an oportunity showed it self our Divsion was the last in here to day we got here about 2 oclk and the first thing was for everry one as soon as unsaddling was to plunge into the River and came back to camp with cleaner bodys than we went in with Our Cavalry is crossing the river here now on transport to join Grants Army but where they are I do not know for I have not seen only 1 News paper thiss month and we recieved some mail to day but there was none for Nelson I have had only 1 letter from home since we left Culpeper and it is nerly 2 months I do think you could write a little oftener. thiss is the first chance I have had of sending anny mail thiss month or I would of writen oftener. Well it is geting nearly dark and

I will close thiss give my love to all I
am well tought and hearty and in good
spirits for our Army is giveing the Rebs
just what they desserve thiss Rebelion
must and shall be Chrushed at anny
sacrifice. Well no more at presant from
your Brother Nelson Taylor
write soon soon

9 N.Y. Cavalry Alens Point James River
June 29
Sister Han

As I have nothing of importance on hand to do thiss afternoon I thought it best to write a few lines for you at home I recieved your letter of May 16th 2 days ago and was glad to learn that you wer all well at home. We are haveing a few days of rest and from all appearances will remain encamped here for a number of days to come to Recruit and rest ourselfs & horses preparatory of making another Raid on some point in Rebeldom again I presume. We are now on the South Bank of the James River our Brigade crofsed yesterday we crofsed on Steam Ferry Boats and it is slow work to Ferry a Corp of Cavalry and to day is the 5th day of crossing and they are nearly all across now.

July 1st I commenced thiss letter 2 days ago and got thiss far and the ever readey Bugler at Division Head Quarters blew Boots & Saddles and everry Buglar in the Divission Repeated the same and we Saddled & marched. I think Gen. Grant is not going to let us have anny rest untill the Richmond question is settled witch perhaps will be one or more months yet for what I know but then I cant tell anything about that strange things hapens in war times. Well we marched from Alans Point out to Prince George C. H. we arrived there about 10 PM and the order was to stand to Horse when we have thoes orders we are suposed to be ready to mount our Horses at anny time when it is necessary but instead of standing to Horse we fasten the Bridle to our leg or arm and roll up in our Rubber Blanket to keep the dew off of us with a stone or Block of wood for a Pillow and enjoy sleep as only a Soldier can. Well I supose you will say I should be afraid of the Horses steping on me but there is no danger of a horse steping on anny one that been in the servis a little while I never had one to tread on me yet Well we slept till sunrise and we fed our Horses & cooked Coffee if it was not for Coffee I do no know what we would do it is half of a soldiers liveing we are in the poorest Country for Water that we have found in the state it is low and swampy and the swamps are nearly dryed up now we are haveing the dryest time I ever saw I think We put 2 or 3 spoons full of dry Coffee in our Canteens and fill it up with Water and let it soak 1 hour and it makes as good a cup of Coffee as if it had been boilled. Well we marched from the C.H. out on to the Petersburgh & Jerusalum Plank Road and camped for the night and we saddled again thiss morning and moved about 3 miles and halted and remained Saddled I presume they exspected an attacked but none was made we are unsaddled and camped for the night we are a litte West of South of Petersburgh an as near as I can learn our troops have nearly surrounded Petersburgh or near enough so the rebs cannot Retreat out of it with anny kind of safety and Grant is Siegeing the place You wanted to know if Gen Sherridan was our Gen yes he comands the Cavalry Corp he has 3 Divisions 1st Brigade Gen Torbart comands 2nd Gen Greg 3^{d} Gen Wilson You wished to know when my time was up the 10th day of Sept I will be 3 years a Soldier but will not get Discharged untill the 2nd day of Oct the Date of organizeation of the company runs out then. Well I have not time to write anny more at presant as the maill is going now and thiss is the 3 time I have taken up the paper and Pencil and thiss is the 2nd day of July and a verry Hot one to

Send me some stamps I have only one left write soon give my love to all the family your Brother

N. Taylor

Camp 9. N.Y. Cavalry near City Point Va
July 8th 1864

Sister Hannah

Well I dont see but I have to do the most of the writeing and so I concluded I had better write again to day as I have plenty of time for writeing although it is verry Hot and dry and the Flies bother one so he can barely do that I wrote you a letter July 2nd We wer then on the Petersburgh Plank Road the next day we came back to thiss place 2 miles from City Point and 1 mile from the James River and camped on a large Plantation where we have a plenty of good spring water witch is a valueable thing in thiss part of Va The Army is haveing a day of rest at presant and perhaps not much will be done thiss month I see in the papers that the Rebs are makeing a Raid up in Maryland but have not had the particulars as yet but I think they will find a few Yanks up there to give them a warm reception The 3^{d} Division of our Cavalry comanded by Gen. Wilson met with quite a loss last week he went out to destroy the Richmond and Danville R. Road and he suceeded in destroying over 20 miles of it and a lot of carss 1 Engine Black smiths shops Saw mills and Watter tanks along the road and on his return he found that he was confronted by a force of Infantry and Cavalry to stop his comeing back and they fought untill they saw that they could not get out and save the Artillery and train and they Spiked there cannon and destroyed there train except 25 Ambulances with wounded fell in the rebs hands thiss was in the night they done it and as near as I can find out everry Regt went for themselves The Rebs wer on 3 sides of them and a large woods and swamp on the 4th side and they took through that in the night and they reached our lines the next day the Division lost about 6 hundred men 12 pieces of Artillerry 30 wagons 25 Ambulances and the number of Horses I do not know. You will see thiss is one of the fortunes of War but the damage don the Rebs will cover our loss in a military point of view. We are liveing on the top shelf at presant haveing to manny good things for our own benefit I think we are haveing a good suply of Vegetables Potatoes Onions Cabage String Beans Cucumbers Pickels Dried Apples Soft Bread and Black Berrys just as manny as one is a mind to pick for there is hundreds of acres black with them We occasionly run

on to a patch of Potatoes and it is
imposible nearly for a Soldier to keep out
of a Potatoe hill if there is anny thing
there large enought to eat and all we are
in want of now is a good Shower of rain
for it does seem as if everrything would
perrish.

 I have nothing more to write at presant
give my respects to all and write soon
from your Broth
N. Taylor
P.S. I see you made a little mistake in
directing your last letter. Direct 9 N.Y.
Cavalry Co I 1st Division 2nd Brigade
Army Potomac

9 N.Y. Cavalry City Point August 1st 1864
Sister Han
 I have a verry few moments to spend
just now and I thought I must improve them
by writeing to you at Home to inform you
of my whereabouts that I am well now. Our
Cavalry Corps has been on the War path
since the 26th. We marched from our
camp and crossed the Appomatac went up the
south side of the James River to near
Akins landing and crossed over to the
north side of the James on the morning 27
and marched up the river 2 miles and not
far from fort Darling and camped there
that night the next morning 28 we wer
attacked by two Divisions of Infantry of

H.P. Hills Corp Rebles the Battle lasted about 2 hours Our Division and the 2nd Division was engadge the Rebs out numbered us 2 to 1 we wer Dismounted and formed a line of Battle the Rebs came on to us with 2 lines of Battle with fixed Bayonet they thought Cavalry would not stand bayonet chardge we lay partly concealed soon as they wer near enought we opened on them with our Carbiens & Revolvers the most of our Cavalry is armed with Spencers Repeating Rifles fire 8 shots without loading they did not come far before they give way and we after them we kild over 300 took 5 hundred prisonerss our loss kild wounded and missing not 2 hundred in the 2 Divisions The 9th N.Y. has another deed of Bravery awardded here in the engagement our Regt captured 65 prisoners and 1 Battle flag from the 28 S. C. Regt S. L. Mallacks of our Company had his Carbine 2 foot from the Collor bearrers head and Ordered him to surrender his answer was never he droped dead before the words fairly left his mouth the Flag was new it has the names of 17 battles witch the regt had been in Mallacks has been promoted to Corpl the Rebs only fired one volley at us without much effect and before they had time to load we wer mixed up with them useing our Revolvers with such slaughter they broke and ran we followed them verry near 1/2 mile and held the Battle field our Regt lost 1 man kild and 2 wounded We recrofsed the river the 29 at dark at daylight we wer crofsing the Appomatac and went out on the lef of oour line and came here last night Our Division is getting a load of Transports here at City point our Brigade embarks thiss afternoon our Destination I presume is Baltimore or Washington to look after the Rebs in Maryland Well I have not time for writeing anny more at presant I presume when you her from me again I will be in Maryland or West Va give my love to all from your Broth

                    Nelson Taylor

Direct to
Co   I   9   N.Y. Cav 1st Division 2nd Brigade Washington D.C.

SHENANDOAH VALLEY CAMPAIGN

Major General Philip H. Sheridan was assigned to command the Army of the Shenandoah. The main object was to coordinate operations against Early's Confederate force. To the Infantry was added Torbert's division of cavalry with him as chief. The cavalry marched all day on the 9th of August, 1864, crossing on a pontoon bridge at Harper's Ferry and camping on the Winchester Turnpike to Halltown. Sheridan's force that he could take into the field was about 26,000.

On August 10 Torbert's cavalry left camp moving through Charlestown and Berryville and going into position near White Post. The 9th N.Y. went on picket near a stone church about four miles south of Berryville. On the 12th the cavalry, after skirmishing with the enemy, moved out on the Front Royal road. The next day the 9th went on picket toward Cedarville. The wagon train of about 300 wagons was loaded with supplies, the mail for the brigade, and the paymaster with $125,000 in United States money with which to pay the brigade. Most of the train passed Berryville with the last fifty wagons pulling out when Moseby with about 200 mounted men charged the rear of the train and captured about 400 mules and horses, many of the teamsters, and the mail. Though the paymaster's box was not taken, the horses were taken from the wagon which was set on fire.

To strengthen his position, Sheridan decided to move back to Halltown. Grant had ordered the cavalry to burn all hay and wheat south of a line from Millwood to Winchester, and to seize all mules, horses, and cattle which might be useful to the army. No houses were to be burned, and the people were to be informed that the object was to make the valley untenable for Confederate raiding parties. The enemy had increased in force at Front Royal and the cavalry was skirmishing every day.

On the morning of August 18, the 9th N.Y. lay in a grove near a stone church south of

Berryville. On the 19th, the 9th N.Y. charged the line of Breckenridge's forces with great success. Near Shepherdstown, the 9th got a fresh supply of ammunition, dismounted, and fought on foot. (Martin Harmon, the Company I friend of Nelson's, and the man who wrote letters to Shubael when Nelson was ill in June and July of 1862, was wounded in the fighting near Leetown.)

From Shepherdstown the 9th moved successively to Harper's Ferry, Charlestown, escorted a train to Ripley, back to Charlestown and Berryville, White Post, Front Royal, across the Opequon to Brucetown and the Winchester Turnpike, Smithfield, Bunker Hill, Mill Creek on the Martinsburg Pike, Steven's Ford, and Charlestown, picketing and/or fighting in these moves.

Nelson was sent to Dismounted Camp arriving there on the 16th of September because his horse had sprained a foreleg and was unfit for duty.

9 N.Y. Cavalry near Charlestown Va.
Shenandoah Valey August 9th
Sister Han

In my last letter I said that we wer going to Marryland. We left City Point the 3rd and landded in Washington the 5th and camped near the City one day and drew what Clothing and other Equipements we wanted and marched again the 6th we came up through Marryland to Harpers Ferry and camped ther last night and crofsed the Potomac thiss morning and we are camped on the Winchester Pike now We marched again in the morning with 3 days Rations and they are to last us 5 days we exspect to have some fighting and no small amount of

marching to do perhaps more marching than fighting There is a large force of Rebs in the Valley about Whinchester. Gen Sherridan is in comand of thiss Department now and we exspect to have some hard fighting to do soon. Well I must stop writeing for it is geting dark I have no light I will close thiss by saying that I am well and hopeing thiss may find you the same at home write as soon as conveniant I recieved a letter from Emma and Frank have not had time to answer it no more at presant give my love to all from your Broth.
          Nelson Taylor

    Camp 9 N.Y. Cavalry Near Front Royal Va
                 Augt 15th
Sister Hannah & Lant
    I recieved your letter some 10 moments ago and as I have nothing to do at presant I thought it best to write you a few lines to inform you that I am alive and well at presant We are within a few miles of Front Royal. I did not exspect to get a letter to day for the Rebs captured a part of our Brigade Suply Train day before yesterday betweeen here and Harpersferry we lost 3 days mail for the Brigade that was on the Train There was some 6 hundred Wagons in the train our Divisions train and some of the Infantry

train Mosby Band atacked it and burnt 40 of our Brigade wagons loaded with grain and Comesarys and ran the Mules off I wrote you a letter the 9 of this month wer then thiss side of Harpers Ferry we marched the 10 up the Valey Our Division had a fight the 11 near Midleton not far from here only one Squadron of our reg was engaged had 2 men wounded. The 3 Brigade Regulars done the most of the fighting we wer fighting the Rear Guard of Earlys forces The Army is laying still here now but how long I cannot say the Weather is hot and dry we have good watter anny amount of Sulphur Springs around where we are. I prefer Soldiering in Western than Eastern Va You said you dident believe I cared annything about comeing home or as much as you did to have me come Well now perhaps I care as much as you do but it is not best for a soldier to look ahead far for Earthly pleasures and enjoyements for we do not know what the morrow may bring forth You wished to know if there was anny propects of the war ending soon I dont see the end yet but I see the prospects are good for War and hard times yet for years to come

Well Lant if your little Girl is as pretty as her name she must be good lookeing I would like to see her and you too for it is a long time since we saw each other

nearly 4 years I believe but I am in hopes that my life may be spared to serve my time and to see you all again give my love to all write soon from your Broth
Nelson Taylor

Shepardstown Va August 23^d 64
Dear Father
As I have only a few moments to write before the mail goes out I cannot write much only to say that I am well at presant The Rebs are going into Marryland again. We wer paid 4 months Pay the 16th I thought it best to send some of it home and enclosed you will find 25 dollars
We had a fight the 16th near Front Royal the same day we wer paid and had another Sunday at Berrywile our forces had a battle yesterday at Charlestown the Rebs are crofsing the River above us and are fighting now I have not time to write anny more now I will write again soon from your son N. Taylor

Camp 9 N.Y. Cav Bolivar Heights near Harpers Ferry August 27th 1864
Sister Han
I seat myself in the shade of a white oak thiss afternoon to write you a short letter & perhaps I may make a long one of it before I finish it. When I wrote you last we wer at or near Front Royal we wer

paid 4 months pay the next day and went out on Picket and the Rebs atacked our line and had a hard Battle for a time & repulsed them and held the field. Only a part of our Regt was engadge our squadron was out on the flank Picketing our Regt lost quite a number that day Well the next morning we retreated back down the Valey to Berryville and had Orders to Burn all Hay & Grain in the Valley it was a hot dry day and the smoke from the thousands of stacks of Hay Wheat & Oats Barns fild with Hay and grain and medows of unmown hay all enveloped in flames Well it looked the most like war of anny time that I have seen yet. We camped at Berryville untill the 21st & wer atacked by Earlys advanceing colums & skirmished with them a little and retreated back to Charlestown two men of our Co Wounded slightly that day We camped that night at Charlestown the next morning we started for Shepardstown at sunrise and soon discovered a colum of Reble Cavalry makeing for the same place marching paralel with us at times from ¼ to ½ mile apart we had the Road and inside track and came in ahead of them Gen Willsons Divsion was in the rear of ours and the Rebs pitched in to him but soon got all the fight they wanted and fell back I wrote a letter to father ther 23^{d} we wer

then near Shepardstown I sent him 25
Dollars When I wrote we heard the Rebs
wer crofsing the Potomac going into
Marryland but there is no force of rebs
north of the Potomac at presant and hardly
think they will atempt to go over there at
thiss presant time. On the Morning 25th
Our Division & the 3^d Divis Willsons Div
came from Army Potomac after we did We
went out from Shepardstown on the
Martinsburgh Pike on a reconnoisance in
force we went out about 6 miles and ran
onto Breckenridges Corp of Infantry and
drove in there Pickets and stired them up
and the Yankees had all they wanted to do
to get out of there way they folowed us
back to Shepardstown and from there down
to Boliver heights where we are now We
had some as Hot work that day as we ever
had Our Capt was wounded verry bad with a
musket Ball in the side. Ed. Lawerance
Kild Martin Harmon Wounded the Regt lost
16 men kild wounded & mifsing Lieut J.
Burroughs kild he was wounded the 1st of
August a year ago came back to the Regt
when we left Culpeper last spring and was
wounded in the first fight we had 7 of may
he got well again came back to the regt
the first of thiss monsth and was wounded
in the fight daybefore yesterday and lived
about 8 hours his brother is first lieut
of our Company. We are camped now about 2

miles up the River from Harpers Ferry the Rebs atacked our troop at Halltown yesterday afternoon had hard fighting for a few hours the enemy fell back at dark and it is all quiet along the lines today I had a letter from Orlando a few days ago It was writen last month they wer all right when he wrote. I wrote him a letter a few days ago. Thiss is the best contry we have been into for Soldiering   Plenty of fruit & Vegtable and occasionly a loaf of Home made Bread. Butter is an article that is allmost entirely forgoten by Soldiers. but if a soldier gets his eye on a loaf of Homemade bread he gets it if Money will get it Well it is geting most dark and the mail goes out early in the morning and I will have to stop writeing for I am rather sleepy was on Picket last night write as soon as you get thiss give my love to all from your broth
     Nelson Taylor

   Smithfield Va Sept 14th 64
Sister Han
  I recieved your letter of the first of thiss month in due time sayeing that the money I sent had arived safely also that you wer all well & going to Campmeting to be gone a number of days Well your letter found me well as usual and in the Sadle most of the time untill a

few days ago while out on a Reconnoisance my Horse Sprained his fore leg and rendered him unfit for duty at presant & perhaps will be so for weeks. We have some rough Rocky roads to march over in thiss Contry & Troopers are not anny to carefull with Uncle Samuels Horses Wel I supose you are exspecting to see me home soon. I will get home sometime next month if nothing happens We will be relieved from the field the 2nd of October and then it will be two or three weeks then before I can get around no doubt We are haveing verry disagreable weather with us at presant heavey rains and quite cool & windy We have been into one fight since I wrote to you before on the 29 of last month here on the same ground where we are camped now our regt lost quite a number We are camped about 18 miles from Harpers ferry. I saw the 49 N.Y. a few days ago I saw Simmons & Jones they wer well I had a letter from Orlando a few days since he is in the Hampton Hospitol Wounded Well I have not much to write about to day it is raining to hard I will call it a letter and let it go out that I am well and tought geting fat as a Pig good by from
      Nelson Taylor

Dismounted camp Md Sept 19th 64
Sister Han

I thought it best to write a few lines thiss morning to inform you where I am and what I was doeing &ce In my last letter I wrote you I said my Horse was unservisable I was sent off to the Dismounted Camp & arived here the 16th and turned over my Horse & Equipements and think it verry probable that I will serve the remainder of my time out here in thiss camp   Our camp is about 4 miles from Harpers Ferry in Pleasant Valey Md. We have two hundred New Recruits here for our Regt 1 Year Men Recruits are comeing in verry brisk at presant Our Division has about 8 hundred Dismounted men camped here Recruits & Old Soldiers Dismounted camp is one of the evils of the Army and there is a class of men that manage some way to get Dismounted and go off to Dismounted camp they call them Dead Beets, Playouts, Bummers &ce. The first night I came in here some of them stole my Harversack I had my Portfolio Housewife and all of my little keepsakes that I had wer in it it was not the value of the articles that I care for because they wer not worth much only I had careyed them ever since I been in the Servis the Testament that Mother gave me when I was home was in it with the rest. Well I dont know as I have annything more to write about at presant Well I exspect to get home sometime next month by the 15 or 20th and sooner if I can If you write again and I guefs you had better Direct in the following

    Nelson Taylor
    Co I 9 N.Y. Cavalry Camp Reemount
    Pleasant Valey Maryland

          Camp Remount Md Sept 24th 64
Sister Han
    I thought it best to write you a few lines again to day in Order to pass away the time. Knowing that you would be glad to hear from me as often as I could write. In the first place I am well and enjoyeing all nefsary comforts of a Soldiers liveing. I supose you have heard of Gen Sherridans great Victory here in the Valey. The Victory is a complete succefs to our army. Our Divisions had an active part in the Battle of Monday Brigd Gen. Merritt comands the Div and the Division Chardged through ther lines of Infantry and captured 750 prisoners 2 pieces of Artilery & 8 Battle Flags Our Regt was in the charge and lost 15 men & 3 Officers kild & Wounded Major Ayers was kild and Capt Rulaford & Wolley were wounded 1 Sergent & 1 private of our company wer wounded Capt Wolley was assigned to duty in our company shortly after Capt Mason

was wounded and he was well liked by the company Our Army is up the Valey 60 miles and it is reported here to day they had a Battle yesterday at Fishers Hill above Strasburg and Defeated Earlys forces again captureing 16 pieces canon and a large number of priseners Well my time has verry near expired 7 days more only but I cant tell how long it will be before I will get my papers I presume not till the excitement is over in the Valey and things get settled a little We moved our camp yesterday and are camped nearer to Harpers ferry 120 men Recruits and 5 of us Old Trooppers are Detailed for Provost duty Provo Guards about the Department here and I exspect we will be on the same duty untill I get out of the servis I think I have writen enought for thiss time from your Broth

     Nelson Taylor
     Camp Remount Md
     9 N.Y. Cavalry

 Camp Remount Md Oct 2nd 64
Sister Han

  I presume by the time thiss reaches you you will be anxiously looking for me home. Well my time is out to day but I have not got my Papers yet but I exspect to have them soon The Officers in charge of the camp has sent to the Regt for our

Descriptive List and as soon as they are sent here we will get our Discharge At presant there is no regular communication with Sherridans Army we have not heard from them since they wer at Staunton and they are suposed to be at or near Lynchburgh and it may be 1 or 2 weeks before my papers will get around I will report myself at C.P. as soon as I am at liberty to do so but do not look for me untill you see me comeing for I dont know myself when I will come. I am well at presant and have good comfortable quarters &ce The past week I have been Drilling Recruits We are haveing fine weather here with us I do not think of annything more at presant from your Broth
   Nelson Taylor
   Camp Remount Pleasant Valey Md
   9 N.Y. Cavalry

   Camp Remount Md Oct 15th 64
Dear Father
  I presume you are looking for me home now everry day. I have not got my Discharge yet I was relieved from duty the 2nd of this month when my time was out and I can not get my Discharge untill the last Companys time is out and that is the 2nd or 5th of next month when all of the old men time is out and then we will all be mustered out together. We are in

Lynchburgh and it may
be 1 or 2 weeks before my
papers will get around
I will report myself at
C. P. as soon as I am at
liberty to do so but do
not look for me until
you see me comeing for
I dont know myself when
I will come. I am well at
present and have good
comfortable quarters &c
The past week I have been
Drilling Recruits
We are haveing fine weather
here with us I do not think
of annything more at prese[nt]
from your Broth[er]

Nelson Tayler

Camp Remount Pleasant
Valey Md Co I 9 N.[Y.]

good quarters and have no duty to do
Rations a plenty Our Regt is out to the
front and the boys are relieved about as
fast as there time is out and sent back
here some coming in most every day There
is no prospects of my geting home before
next month now but I will come as soon as
I can I am well at presant   from your son
        Nelson Taylor
        Pleasant Valey
        Camp Remount Md 9 N.Y. Cavalry

              Baltimore Oct 30 1864
Dear Father
    I recieved my Discharge yesterday
morning at Harpers Ferry and came here to
Baltimore last night to late to get my Pay
& concequently I have to lay over untill
Monday I will get my pay and leave here
tomorrow night I will stop in New York a
few days before I come home I am well no
more at presant
              from your son
              N Taylor

To whom it may Concern

Know ye, That Nelson Taylor a Corporal of Captain H. W. Mason Company L, Ninth Regiment of New York Cavalry VOLUNTEERS, who was enrolled on the tenth day of September one thousand eight hundred and sixty one to serve three years or during the war, is hereby **Discharged** from the service of the United States this twenty fifth day of October 1864, at Middletown Virginia by reason of Expiration of term of Service. (No objection to his being re-enlisted is known to exist.)

Said Nelson Taylor was born in Saratoga in the State of New York, is 25 years of age, 6 feet 2¼ inches high, light complexion, Blue eyes, Black hair, and by occupation, when enrolled, a Farmer.

Given at Middletown Va. this Twenty fifth day of October 1864.

Geo. S. Nichols
Lt. Col.
Commanding the Reg't.

*Baltimore Oct 31, 1864
Paid L. L. Par of public and $100 U.S. Bounty
Geo. W. Carpenter*

APPENDIX

AFTERTHOUGHT - (After Discharge)

What happened to Nelson Taylor after his discharge? We know that he returned home to Clifton Park on November 5, 1864. Subsequent information is sketchy and comes mainly from a few letters, from town and city directories, and listings in the 1865 and subsequent censuses.

1865 - The census for this year states that Nelson, 26, formerly in the Army is living with his brother, George W. Taylor and family on George's farm in Clifton Park.

1866 - As above.

1867 - Harmony Mills (Knitting) was built in Cohoes. This is important because of Nelson's reference in a letter dated June 18, 1867, to his "lady love," Marietta Lighthall, "After I left you at the mill yesterday..." Marietta must have been employed there. Nelson Taylor is listed as a policeman boarding at 24 Canal Street, Cohoes.

Three letters from Nelson to Marietta have been preserved. He addresses her as "Mate," pronounced perhaps as "Matty," or "Mate" as in "shipmate."

Cohoes March 14th 67

Friend Mate

I said thiss noon that if you would call at the Post Office thiss evening you would find a note letting you know wether I could go to the Party to night or not I am sorry to say that I cannot get excused from duty to night. I am sorry because I wanted to go, verry much but cannot without Disobeying Orders, and do not want to do that.

I will see you again soon and will tell you more about it than what I can write yours in haste
from your friend

       Nelson Taylor

     Green Island June 18th
Dear Mate

 I promised you yesterday that I would write you a note or rather a letter and it is so still quiet & lonely here on the Island to day, and I have been reading and sleeping and thinking so I thought I would put some of my thoughts on paper and send them to you. My Dearest I belive thiss is the first letter I have written to you with the exception of a note or two preveious to thiss. And I will tell you before hand that I am a porr hand to write letters but you would found that to be so without my telling of it. After I left you at the mill yesterday I came down on the Island and stayed till after Dinner then I went over to Troy or rather to North Troy, to my Neices and spent the afternoon, and while there my Broth John & wife and two of ther Daughters came ther and I had a good visit. I presume you thought I was to the Pick Nix yesterday afternoon but I did not go. there was a good many there by the way they went down through here last night from dark untill after 12 oclk. I see hardly anny one here that I know except thoes that are on the Horse Cars, and I dont have anny chance to talk with them. I like my Boarding place well, it is only a few steps from the Station house by the new Church they have 4 men boarders beside me

    Mate if I dont see you again before Sunday I will be up then and if you want to go to your Sisters and me to go I will go I will come up to Cohoes Friday forenoon, and will see you when you come home at noon if nothing hapens I am goeing to send for the Waverly to day.

    I have just had a call from Cohoes John McDermott stoped here to see how we keeped things we have to look out for him as well as the boys in Cohoes do Mate write me a good long letter when you get thiss will you I know you will I will close thiss letter by sayeing to you accept thees few lines from one that loves you, honestly, and with pure motives. write soon

                      Yours truly
                        N Taylor

            Green Island June 26th 67

Dear Mate

    It is with pleasure that I write you a few lines thiss morning as I promised to do when I was with you Sunday but I hardly know what to write about because we have no news here on the Island of anny importance, more than it is verry warm weather dry & dusty

  I was up to Cohoes yesterday afternoon but went nowhere but to the Station House. I went up after some of my clothes. I wish that I knew whether I was goeing to stay here or not so I could get my things all together, but such is life and I will have to bear with it I attended a Strawbery Festival Monday eve at the new church and got some Strawberys & Ice cream and did not see but one person in the the church that I knew and that was the Lady that I boarded with last week, so I had to enjoy the berrys & cream alone and I left as soon as I got through I was only away from the Station 20 moments. by the way I went a fishing yesterday had grand luck caught one herring & one Bullhead and lost my knife in the bargain the fish I threw back in the river so you see it is profitable to go a fishing. I shall exspect to see you down here Friday night unless I here from you to the contrary I hardly think I shall get up to Cohoes again before that time but write and let me know all the news & come down on the 8 oclk car and I will get on the car somewhere in the vilage.

> I saw Frank Cole and H. Fonda Sunday eve goeing over to West Troy. Frank asked me if I had been up to see Mate to day I said yes.
>
> I think of nothing more to write thiss morning and I will close I still remain your friend and lover write soon
>
> N Taylor

Nelson Taylor and Marietta Lighthall were married on May 6, 1868, by Rev. Charles Waldron. (My father, Charles Waldron Taylor, was named for him.)

Their first child, Amelia, was born on October 18, 1869, in Marshalltown, Iowa, according to baptismal records of the Cohoes Dutch Reformed Church. A second child, Shubael, was born in Marshalltown on December 9, 1870.

The directory for Marshalltown, Iowa, for the years 1869-71 lists Nelson as resident and laborer.

The 1872 Green Island, NY, directory records Nelson Taylor as "Stove mounter" living at 56 George Street.

On March 17, 1873, Charles Waldron Taylor was born in Green Island; and in that year on November 16, Amelia died.

On May 10, 1874, Shubael and Charles were baptized. Nelson Taylor was listed in the directory as "Policeman," living on Schuyler Street near Congress Street in Cohoes.

From 1874 through 1886 he was on the police force in Cohoes, NY serving as "Acting sergeant of police" in 1877.

In 1879 Nelson's mother, Alida Teachout Taylor died, On April 7, 1881 Nelson Armsby Taylor was born and was baptized on May 25. On June 30 of that year, Nelson's father, Shubael, died at age 84.

The 1887 Cohoes directory lists Nelson as "Confectionery" at 163 Remsen Street with home address of 173 Main Street.

On July 3, 1888, Nelson Taylor was appointed Chief of Police in the city of Gloversville, New York, and organized its police force. He died in service on August 22, 1898.

PLATE XV

WEDDING PHOTO OF NELSON
AND ALIDA TEACHOUT

PLATE XVI

GLOVERSVILLE NY CHIEF OF POLICE
NELSON TAYLOR

PLATE XVII

GLOVERSVILLE POLICE FORCE HEADING A
FUNERAL PROCESSION - CHIEF NELSON
TAYLOR AT LEFT

THE GETTYSBURG REUNION - JULY 1,2,3, 1893

In his book "History of the Ninth New York Cavalry, War of 1861 to 1865," Newell Cheney relates that the New York State Legislature of 1886 passed an act providing for securing and permanent marking of the movements and positions of the New York State troops at Gettysburg. An appropriation of $1,500 was authorized for the erecting of monuments for each regiment and battery.

On October 2 and 3, 1886, the survivors of the 9th N.Y. Cavalry celebrated at Westfield, NY the 25th anniversary of its organization and formed a regimental association through which $845 was added to the $1,500 given by the State for the 9th N.Y. Cavalry monument on the Gettysburg battlefield.

The Association approved two inscriptions: "Discovering the Enemy" and "Picket on Chambersburg road fired on at 5 a.m. July 1." At first there was strong objection by the Battlefield Memorial Association on the ground of not being historically correct. However, evidence was presented so convincingly that the Memorial Association voted to allow the inscriptions and the published proceedings state, "At a meeting held July 3, 1888, a committee of the Ninth New York Cavalry appeared before the board, and established to the entire satisfaction of those present that this regiment fired the first shot of July 1, 1863."

The 30th reunion of the 9th was certainly an important one for the veterans of the engagement, and Nelson attended. We are fortunate to have his letter of June 30, 1893 written home to family concerning this reunion.

Getysburgh Pa June 30 - 93

Dear Wife & Boys

I arrived in New York at Ma House at 3.45 P.M. the Day I left Home & left there at 3.15 the 29 went over to Jersey City & took the Leigh Vally Road at 6 P.M. and arrived in Harrisburgh at 12 midnigh could not get a Train out untill 8.05 in the morning I stoped at the Commercial Hotel and left Harrisburgh at 8.05 and got in Gettysburg at 10.10 and found a Private Boarding House $1.50 Per Day nearly every House in town is a Boarding House 4 of us in a Room 26 New York old Vets and one old Vet of a Pa Reg I met on the Train and have 3 good men in our Room well there is a lot of old Vets here and every train are loaded with them I have met Several of 9 Boys but none of my old co yet MaMa it is Just Splendid to meet the old Boys I am goeing to see the the old Places after Dinner. no more at Present love to all from your old hubby

N. Taylor

REPORT OF REUNION OF CAVALRY ATTENDED BY NELSON TAYLOR

Gettysburgh June 30th 93
12.30 P.M.

P. K. Benson 50 Pa In Reg and myself went into the National Cemetary and out on the line of the Battle ground of the last Day fight down to the Little Round Top and to the Divels Den and Returned to our Boarding House at 6.30 P.M. I passed over the ground that General Picket & his men made there Desperat Charge July 3rd it is a grand seen for ann old Soldier who was there 30 years ago Some of the Regt Monuments are Splendid and there is more to be errected I met Several comrads of our old Regt but none of Co I.

Saturday July 1 1893 I was up and out at 5 A.M. walk up on Cemetary Hill Several Hundred of the old comrads Sleped in Tents last night I am not well thiss morning Played out Started out and met comrad W. T. Bradshaw - Denvenport Capt Leapham Capt Robertson and met about 70 of the 9th Boys none of Co I could not stay out had to come back to my Boarding House took a Rest for an hour went down on the Dimond and met for the first time since the 30th day of October 1864 a comrade of my old co Robert M. Hall & James Wallace (alias Tonkey) Visited with them a while and returned to Boarding House for a rest

1P.M. Myself & Comrade Wallace went out on the Mumetburg Road where our Old Regt first went into action I remembered the location & the lay of the Country verry well I cut a Hickery Stick on the Ground where we first went into the fight & I cut a Sprig off of a Gum Tree where the first Rebel Prisoner was Captured at Gettysburg by Perry Nichols of Co F at 5

A.M. on the farm Owned & Occupied then and now by Forney. When the Rebls first began to Shell us one of there Shells went through one corner of his House and he has the Shell laying in his Door yard now he has a Piece of Tin nailed over the holes made by the Shell near the Place I cut the Hickory Stick the first Union Soldier Kild at Gettysburg was Corporal Cyrus James of Co. G 9 N.Y. Cavalry At 4 P.M. we had a Reuinon at our Monument about 30 of the old comrads wer there Capt Bache & Wife & Son Capt Goodrich Capt Dicksen Capt Robertson Capt Cheeny & others Capt Wooley Capt Bache Son took a Photo of uss in front of our Monument At 7.30 P.M. our Regt had a Reunion at the M. E. Church on East Midle Stt About 70 Present It was ann event in our lives that we never can forget it was well worth all it cost to come here

Sunday July 2nd 93
Breakfast 6 A.M. I went out over Culps Hill to the extreme Right of our lines Saw a Batery of Regular 4 Pieces in camp 10.15 A.M. the Batery fired 4 Rounds Saw the reunion of the 12th Corps General Slocum & General Warren of the 12 Corps made addresses Gover Flower & Staff of N.Y. were there Flower Delivered an address. I got a Drink out of Spangless Spring where the Rebs & Yanks both Drank

together on the night of July the first I
cut a Hickory Stick under the Oak Tree
where a Rebel Sharp Shooter was Stationed
in Front of the 150 N.Y. infantry on Culps
Hill July the Second he was Straped to
the Tree so if he was wounded he would not
fall he was kild by the 15 N.Y. and after
the Batle he was cut down with 12 Bullet
hole through his Body I cut a piece of
Elder on the Ground we occupied about 2.30
P.M. July the first near the Cemetary (and
I went to Dinner 11.30 AM At 1.30 we wer
Ordered to Assemble on Baltemore St to
march to the National Cemetary at the
Dedication of the State Monument There
was 124 comerads of our old Regt Reported
and only 4 of our old Co I Reported it was
a grand Seen to see the Old Vets a few
more than 7,000 Thousand Reported here we
marched into the Cemetary and Massed at
the Monument we wer about 20 feet in front
of the Stand it was very Warm I stood it
for ann Hour and I got so tired wen
General Sickels got through I got out of
the crowd I did not care to hear the rest
of the Speakers and Half or more of the
Vets Started away for another tramp around
the Battle field I went and looked at the
old House that Gen Mead had his
Headquarters Several Shell Holes in it
yet I cut a Small Sliver off of one of

the Holes and I spent the Evning with Dickson Robertson & Hall

Monday July 3 - 93
I bid good by to most of all of the 9 Boys & then took a Ride over the Second & Third Days Battle ground I have a piece of Stone Chiped off of the Devils Denn Rock I picked Some Wheat & Daises near the High Water Mark where Reb General Lewis Armstead was kild at Pickets charge I am goeing to Start for Home this afternoon I left Getysburgh at 6 PM arrived at Allentown Pa at 11 P.M. Stoped over night and arrived Home 8 P.M. July 4th

FROM TAYLOR FAMILY RECORDS

Shubael Taylor bMay 18, 1797 dJune 30, 1881

Alida Teachout Taylor - wife of Shubael
bJune 19, 1801 dJanuary 16, 1879

John S. Taylor - Son of Shubael and Alida
bSeptember 29, 1821 dNovember 21, 1901

George W. Taylor - Son of Shubael and Alida
bApril 17, 1874 dJuly 14, 1901

Lydia Taylor - Daughter of Shubael and Alida
bOctober 13, 1826 dMay 16, 1861

Loantha Taylor - Daughter of Shubael and Alida
bJune 30, 1830 dSeptember 10, 1890
(Frequently referred to as "Lant")

Hannah Taylor - Daughter of Shubael and Alida
bSeptember 8, 1836 d ?

Nelson Taylor - Son of Shubael and Alida
bJanuary 24, 1839 dAugust 22, 1898

MARRIAGES

Shubael and Alida Teachout - October 25, 1820

John S. Taylor and Eliza Walradt - December 5, 1843

George W. Taylor and Esther Traver - December 19, 1848

Lydia Taylor and John B. Walradt -

Loantha Taylor and Abel Baker - January 16, 1855

Hannah Taylor and Hiram Usher - January 28, 1857
"   "   " Adam Mott - January 1, 1877

Nelson Taylor and Marietta Lighthall - May 6, 1868

SOURCE MATERIALS

The sources listed below provided background for commentary on the forces influencing the movements of the 9th NY Cavalry

American Heritage, Editors. The Civil War. c1960. American Heritage Publishing Co., Inc. Two volumes.

Catton. Bruce. Gettysburg - The Final Fury. c1974. Doubleday & Company, Inc., Garden City, NY.

Catton, Bruce. The Army of the Potomac - A Stillness at Appomattox. c1953. Doubleday & Company, Inc., Garden City, NY.

Catton, Bruce. This Hallowed Ground - The Story of the Union Side of the Civil War. c1955. Doubleday & Company, Inc., Garden City, NY.

Cheney, Newell. History of the Ninth New York Volunteer Cavalry, War of 1861 to 1865. Martin Merz & Son, Jamestown, NY (No Copyright imprint).

Dawson, William Forrest, Ed. A Civil War Artist at the Front, Edwin Forbes' Life Studies of the Great Army. c1957. Oxford University Press, Inc., New York, NY.

Kettel, Thomas P. History of the Great Rebellion. Stebbins, Hartford CT. 1866.

Lang, E.B. The Civil War Day by Day - An Almanac 1861 - 1865. Doubleday & Company, Inc., Garden City, NY.

MacDonald, John. Great Battles of the Civil War. c1988. Macmillan Publishing Company, New York, NY.

Rhodes, James Ford. History of the Civil War 1861-1865. c1917. The Macmillan Company, New York, NY. 1933.

Stackpole, Edward J. *They Met at Gettysburg.* c1956, The Telegraph Press, Harrisburg, PA.

Storrick, W. C. *The Battle of Gettysburg.* c1935. J. Horace McFarland Co., Mount Pleasant Press, Harrisburg, PA.

Ward, Geoffrey C. *The Civil War, An Illustrated History.* c1990. Alfred A. Knopf, Inc., New York, NY. 1990.

NEIGHBORS AND FRIENDS MENTIONED

Levi Clapper, Simmons boys   p6
Albert Wells   p10
Eli Weeks, Elisha Morse   p11
Henry Bradshaw   p12
Peter Simmons   pp15, 153, 179
Seth Higgins, Gilbert Clements   p31
Martin Harmon   pp47, 48, 138, 177
Isac Chadsey   p53
Theodore Salsbury   p80
Orlando Swartwout, John Filkins, Peter Butlar   p94
Naham P. Arnold   p106
Perkins, Wadsworth   p114
John Peck Higgins, Wadsworth White   p133
T. G. Histed   p146
Elihu Jones   pp153, 179
S. L. Mallacks   p168
Ed Lawerance   p177
P. K. Benson   p184
W. T. Bradshaw, Robert M. Hall, James Wallace (alias Tonkey), Perry Nichols   p195
Cyrus James   p196

www.ingramcontent.com/pod-product-compliance
Lightning Source LLC
Chambersburg PA
CBHW051045160426
43193CB00010B/1068